BREAKING THE CURSE

BREAKING THE CURSE

A Memoir of Trauma, Healing, and Italian Witchcraft

ALEX DIFRANCESCO

SEVEN STORIES PRESS

New York • Oakland • London

"Sing Another Song, Boys" © 1993 by Leonard Cohen, used by permission of The Wylie Agency LLC; "If I Didn't Have Your Love" © 2016 by Leonard Cohen, used by permission of The Wylie Agency LLC.

"The Guest House" on page 166 and epigraph on page 7 from *The Essential Rumi*, translated by Coleman Barks, copyright © 2004.

Seven Stories Press
140 Watts Street
New York, NY 10013
www.sevenstories.com

Library of Congress Cataloging-in-Publication Data

Names: DiFrancesco, Alex, author.
Title: Breaking the curse : a memoir / by Alex DiFrancesco.
Description: New York, NY : Seven Stories Press, [2024]
Identifiers: LCCN 2023043070 | ISBN 9781644213841 (trade paperback) | ISBN 9781644213858 (ebook)
Subjects: LCSH: DiFrancesco, Alex. | Transgender people--United States--Biography. | Gender nonconforming people--United States--Biography. | Rape victims--United States. | Addicts--Rehabilitation--United States. | Mentally ill--Rehabilitation--United States.
Classification: LCC HQ77.8.D54 A3 2024 | DDC 306.76/8092 B--dc23/eng/20231023
LC record available at https://lccn.loc.gov/2023043070

College professors and high school and middle school teachers may order free examination copies of Seven Stories Press titles. Visit https://www.sevenstories.com/pg/resources-academics or email academic@sevenstories.com.

Printed in the United States of America

9 8 7 6 5 4 3 2 1

For
St. Hildegard of the visions

Don't turn your head.
Keep looking at the bandaged place.
That's where the light enters you.

—RUMI

Works in this book have appeared, in some form, in:

The Rumpus
Olney
beestung
ALOCASIA
Pithead Chapel

An enormous thank you to all the editors of these magazines, Lisa Mecham, Sarah Clark, Lauren Thomas, and Kate Gehan. Writing about trauma is a dangerous thing, and the above magazines and editors inspired my trust.

THIS IS A STORY

From one angle, this story begins when a girl is standing on a cliff, high on cocaine, ready to jump into the turbulent stream at the base of a waterfall. She does not know why she always chooses chaos. Her knees are shaking. She is worried that rocks lie under the roaring water, ready to break her. But she will jump, anyway, and the water will feel like a crystal injection into her mouth and nose, washing the cocaine back and away as her jackhammering heart pumps her high out of her body. From one angle, this is a story of addiction.

■

From another angle, this story begins when a little boy is trying to tell the people around him who he is. They are his family, and they say they love him, but they cannot hear him. They do not hear that he wants to cut off his waist-length hair. They do not hear that he wants to wear sweatpants and sport shirts, not dresses. They do not hear, and when they do, they react in the kind of fear and disgust that makes a person completely forget who they are for decades. From one angle, this is a story about transgender identities.

■

From another angle, this story begins when a young woman is breaking from reality. She is in a dirty apartment in the town she grew up in. She thinks someone has broken into her apartment to write in her journal. She thinks that when she leaves her light on at night, people think it is to bring them to her. She ends up in a mental hospital, and though it is the first time, it will be far from the last.

■

In some ways, this story begins when a nonbinary person is raped for the first time. For the second time. For the third time. For the fourth time. For the fifth time.

■

This is a story of a little girl reading a book of spells, hoping to find love in it.

■

This is a story of a little boy who is told that things he sees, things he knows, are not real. He is told so many times that reality begins to break under the weight of it.

■

If you are following the story of the little trans boy:

A thirty-year-old person lies in bed with their lover, and they talk about everything that they have forced out of their mind. They talk about who they truly are for the first time in twenty-five years. They find acceptance from this lover, and because of that they begin to grow into the person they have hidden for so long. They stop ending up in mental hospitals. And one night, when it is their lover's birthday, they drink just one glass of wine with dinner because everything is okay now. Nothing is okay. In some ways, the story begins again here.

■

If you are following the story of the little trans boy:

The nonbinary person's lover leaves them, and the nonbinary person leaves their home on a train to travel five hundred miles away. Their hair is cut short, and they are in men's clothes while they board the train. They wear an old subway token on a chain, which they will somehow lose in their new home, though they've had it for decades. They are the wildest dream of their child self.

Sometimes, the story begins when they leave the only place that has ever been their home.

■

If you are following the story of rape:

In some ways, this story begins the night they are raped for the fifth time, when they take Xanax after they have been drinking whiskey all night. This is a story about addiction, after all. Maybe you are following the story from the girl on the cliff.

■

If you are following the story of the little trans boy:

Two years after they come out, their lover cums in them without their consent, and they decide that they will never let themselves be surprised by someone they love again, therefore they will never let anyone they love close to them ever again. It doesn't matter if the person is the first one who has ever seen them for who they truly are. Anyone can hurt you. Anyone will hurt you. The little boy cannot know who he is. He cannot put words on what is done.

This is a story about transness, and about rape, after all.

∎

If you are following the story of the fifth rape:

In the years after the night of the fifth rape, the nonbinary person drinks every day, and sometimes trades sex for drugs. This is a story about rape, and about addiction, after all.

∎

If you are following the story of mental illness:

There is an anger that the nonbinary person cannot control, and it spills out and hurts those around them. It gets worse when they descend back into addiction after the fifth rape. This is a story about complex trauma, after all. Or maybe you are following the story of the girl on the cliff. Or maybe you are following the story about rape.

∎

If you are following the story of the fifth rape:

The nonbinary person reports the crime, eventually. When they request the public document of the police report, the details of the rape are blacked out, redacted, just like they are in their memory.

∎

If you are following the story of magic:

The nonbinary person sits in their bedroom, overwhelmed with depression, shuffling their tarot cards again and again, wondering why they are always in the darkest part of the Major Arcana.

■

If you are following the story of the little trans boy:

After the nonbinary person leaves their lover, they begin taking testosterone. They had devoted all their energy previously to their partner's needs. Now they focus on themself. Their voice deepens, slightly; they grow a goatee. They move to a western suburb of Cleveland. They go back to school. They face so much discrimination they didn't even know was there when they lived in New York City with their lover. It gets worse and worse, and their ability to see themselves as worth anything sinks lower and lower. This is when they are raped for the fifth time. This is when they sink back into addiction. This is when the laws begin, first with Trump, then beyond him: the ones that try to eradicate people like them. They go to rehab, eventually, they get dialectic behavioral therapy. They start standing with their spine straight, when before, they had hunched at the shoulders, sinking their breasts in. They get put on an antidepressant. They relapse, a few times, but the things they learn in rehab stick. They begin studying ancient traditions, hoping that they will link them to something. They begin to want to live again. Even when the fifth rapist sues them for defamation, they do not collapse in on themself. They, somehow, amidst all this, begin to be able to accept life.

This is where the story of transness, addiction, mental health, rape, and magic come together, if you were looking for that.

■

This is a story.

This is a story.

This is a story.

This is a story.

This is a story that cannot be told without addiction. It cannot be told without mental illness. It cannot be told without the story of an abused transgender child. What would be so nice is if this was just a story about addiction. Or just a story about mental illness. Or just a story about abuse. Or just a story about gender identity. Or just a story about magic. But none of these stories can be told without telling the others.

This is a story of someone who, despite the Jenga tower of these things, did not collapse. This is, finally, a story about picking the pieces back up.

PART ONE

THE DEVIL .

"The Devil can indicate a narrow materialistic view of life; it can mean any form of misery or depression, especially feeling chained or imprisoned, with the illusion that no alternatives are possible . . . The Devil signifies being a slave of your desires, rather than acting the way you think is best."

—RACHEL POLLACK, *Seventy-Eight Degrees of Wisdom: A Tarot Journey to Self-Awareness*

CLIFF DIVING

A roaring waterfall cascades next to a series of cliffs in Pottsville, Pennsylvania. Down in the water that thunders forward past the waterfall, groups of people are swimming, screaming, laughing in the humid summer air. Up on one of the cliffs stand two girls, seventeen and eighteen, their knees shaking, their bodies and nervous systems amped up on the cocaine they've been snorting in their friend's car. They are both beautiful, though neither of them really accepts or knows that in a fundamental way. They are both dark-haired, Italian, hell-bent on self-destruction. Within two years, both of their fathers will be dead. These girls are wide-eyed, wild, always making the choice towards chaos. The one we will follow: she hates her name, she hates her body, she hates her life when it is restricted in the confines of home, school, work. She likes taking drugs and reading books and watching art house movies and listening to jam bands and classic rock. Within a few years, she will have an angel and a devil tattooed on her back with lines from a Bob Dylan spoken word piece—for the rest of her life, her skin will proclaim, "Your sun-decked deserts and evergreen valleys turn to broken-down slums and trashcan alleys." In a few years, the other girl, recently home from a detention center, will join the air force, be shipped off to Okinawa, meet a husband, have a child, calm down, and begin to live. The girl we will follow is never sure she figures out how to live, not really, though survival becomes something she is quite good at.

They stand on the cliff, shaking, while the girl we will not follow tries to convince the one we will to jump.

"What if there are rocks down there?" the girl we follow shouts over the roar of the water. Death, while attractive, seems less attractive with broken bones, pain, drowning attached to it.

"It's fine!" her friend yells back. "People jump off here all the time."

Their adrenaline is ruining their high, pumping the cocaine through their bodies too fast as their hearts jackhammer in their chests.

"I don't feel so good," the girl says, less loudly than she'd screamed the last question.

"We'll go back and do another line in the car after!" her friend yells. No one hears them below, not over the sound of the falls. "Come on, just jump!"

Her friend tires of the argument and jumps, screaming, off the cliff. The girl, afraid to be seen as afraid, follows a split second later. They hit the water at nearly the same time, and it seems that crystals shoot into their noses, their throats, washing the drip of the cocaine away. Around them, the summer sun makes diamonds in the water that reflect up against the cliffs. They laugh, scream, splash with the people who were beneath them, who are now abreast of them. It seems they can fly. They pull themselves out of the water, onto the rocks, and head back to their friend's car, where with dollar bills and straws and razors and mirrors, they cut more lines, snort them, go back to jump again.

■

When she is seventeen, after a trip to the ocean where she gets an ear infection, she lays in bed for a week, convinced her brain is bleeding, only able to drag herself back and forth to the bathtub and drink orange juice. This episode, when it passes, feels like some sort of trial. She will sleep, wake up as she was before, and think how odd this all was, be glad it is over.

■

The girl does not have a happy life. She was suspended for getting drunk in school while in eleventh grade. She learned that if she wanted to avoid people's questions about whether she was okay— she was not—all she had to do was raise her grades in school and show up every day. It was easy. If you did what you were supposed to in some realms, she found, no one worried about the others. Her home life was difficult—her father and grandmother were ill. When she was fifteen, her mother tried to teach her how to catheter her grandmother while she lay in her hospital bed. She thinks something broke in her then. Her responsibilities were too much. She hid in her room, writing on an old manual typewriter that her mother would always tell her was going to ruin her wrists (it did, eventually, along with all the manual labor she will do for most of her life).

Life is not easy. She goes out on Friday nights all throughout high school and drinks until she vomits off the sides of the porches of friends whose parents are working third shift. She begins to take cocaine, to love its drip down her throat and how it allows her to speak and speak in ways she is often too shy for. She likes the illicit. She likes acid, and mushrooms (which inevitably make her feel like she's going to shit her pants—she takes them anyway), and ecstasy, and pot, and anything she can get her hands on, except for heroin, which even her group of hell-bent friends know is the worst thing, the one you can't come back from.

When she is eighteen, she is set to get on a train and go across the country to a small liberal arts school in Santa Fe which has accepted her on full scholarship. Her mind breaks, and she defers the acceptance until the next semester. She wanders around for three months, drinking in a downtown bar she's far too young to be at, watching all her friends go away to school and start their lives in earnest. Her mother tells her, while she is making plans to leave, that if she leaves she should never come back, not after abandoning her family who needs her. This sounds fine. Her mother seems to think she is barring her from a place she wants to be. Her home has not felt like home for many years, and the idea of losing it does not bother her.

She packs an army duffle bag she got at the Salvation Army and prepares to get on an Amtrak in Philadelphia, where one of her friends will drive her, in early January of her eighteenth year. They get in a car accident on the way, and she decides that this is a sign, it is fate, she was never meant to go. And, so, she retreats into a job as a short order cook in a pizza place, and nights at the bar that serves minors.

∎

The bar downtown that serves minors is dark and smells faintly of age and disrepair. The back room is large, and there are tables where her and her friends sit, playing songs on the jukebox. It is not the modern kind, with access to any song, so they pick out their favorites from the selection that has been there for decades, typed on little white and pink cards, unchanged: "American Pie," "Never Tear Us Apart," "All I Want Is You." There is a poetry reading that happens once a month in this bar, led by an old local poet who rides around town alone on a two-person bicycle, and they go to it every time, reading from their journals, trying to be poets themselves. It is at this poetry reading that the girl meets her first real boyfriend—if you don't count the heroin addict she had a crush on in high school who she dated afterwards for a brief period, who she doesn't count, no matter how big the crush was, no matter that he was the second boy she ever slept with, no matter that the night they slept together, he lit candles in his bedroom and they fell asleep with them still burning and wax cascaded down all the surfaces in his room the next morning, making beauty he cursed at. He does not count. The boy she meets at the poetry reading: for her whole life, she will wonder if he was her one chance at happiness, while knowing she never could have grown into the person she would become if she stayed with him. But this is before all that, this is when he invites her to parties at his house and shows her the sculptures made of broken things that he built in the basement of his parents' house, where he lives. This is when he reads poetry that seems real and good and emotional at the bar once a month. This is when they drink together every night, go back to his basement apartment in his parents' house, watch *Fear and Loathing in Las Vegas*, and have sex. She loves him with all her heart, and it is a fierce and terrifying thing to love with the intensity she finds herself capable of.

She doesn't remember, later, why they fight one night, why they break up, but she knows that she finds herself in the back room of the bar, alone, and then not alone when a boy named Michael shows up. They are, again, two beautiful people, but Michael knows how beautiful he is, and uses it to his advantage all the time. Michael is a junkie. Michael has dated many of the girl's friends and treated them poorly, cheating on them and hitting them. But the girl is sad, the girl is drunk, and when Michael focuses his attractive powers on her, she is not immune. They start talking about drugs, about heroin, Michael's truest love.

The next morning, the girl wakes up in his bed, and he brushes her hair off her face and tells her she is so beautiful, a classic sort of beauty, a Renaissance painting. Would she consider being his muse? Even the then nineteen-year-old girl knows this is bullshit, but they drive to her mother's house anyway, him hiding in the back seat of her SUV as she picks up her work clothes and tells her mother she is heading in for her lunch shift at the fine dining restaurant she'd moved up to from the pizza place.

She calls in sick to work, and they drive down the PA turnpike to Philly. There, they score almost as if by magic. In North Philly, Michael indicates a man on a street corner, they pull up to him, Michael hands him the hundred dollars they've scraped together, he throws them back a bundle of dope. Driving back home, on the turnpike, the girl snorts bumps off the back of her hand while Michael shoots up in the passenger seat. She has never felt so right in her life, so low and beneath everything that troubles her: her dying father and grandmother, her mother's emotional and verbal abuse, her abusive siblings. It is like being alive and dead at once, and the girl loves it. Heroin is the answer she has been looking for, she feels, even though she knows that this is the bad zone that she had promised herself through many coked-out nights she'd never reach. It doesn't matter. Whoever said heroin was bad was a fucking liar. It is exactly what she has always needed.

THE APARTMENT BUILDING AND THE SANTERÍA SHOP

The building was three stories tall and had apartments on every floor except the street-facing part of the ground one, where there were businesses. I didn't notice, then, that the ceiling was collapsing in the third-floor apartment that the realtor showed to me, my eyes going instead to the recently finished floors and the huge amount of closet space he pointed out, rather than the imperfections. This is the way it always is for me. I walk into situations seeing only what others want to me to see. There is a certain sleight of hand that I have to be on guard for, which I seldom am. I trust until there is proof that trust is not deserved. It puts me in a lot of situations I don't care for, but what I would care for much less would be walking through the world with mistrust and prejudice.

This is how it was when I moved to Cleveland, too. I had romanticized the Midwest, its crumbling buildings, its worn-down charm. It reminded me of home, I thought and often said, home being Wilkes-Barre, PA, a failing, decaying coal mining town. The sun would come up over the Cuyahoga River, and I'd drive across the sun-gold expanse of the water, over the bridge with its solemn guardian statues, seeing smoke billowing from factory buildings, ruins in the morning mist. There was something beautiful about it, then. Something that filled me with hope and joy. There were times that I thought I'd live there forever. There were times I thought I'd build community. There were times when I believed the enthusiasm of the people who loved the city desperately, despite how they walked around in shirts with Cleveland emblazoned across the front, cheesily, like tourists, claiming Cleveland was "the best city in the world," though they clearly had not seen much of the rest of the world. It was like home, I said, forgetting that I had left home long ago, for good reason.

I lived in Little Italy for around a year, in a back apartment of a building that, when fumigated, had insects that looked prehistoric lumber out of the walls. My neighbors were mostly old Italian men who hated minorities, myself included. My windows in my apartment were painted shut and the walls were thin, without insulation, as hot in the summer as living in a tent, and as cold in the winter as sleeping in a car. When I finally left, it was because a ground-level, painted-shut window had smashed when I tried to open it, the super hadn't bothered putting a new one in, and the fleas from the cats that lived in the shed out back infested my apartment and my cat. I left the apartment like I'd found it, but worse: the sink full of dishes, the things I didn't want any more piled on the floor.

Then, I was moving to the suburb on the West Side that everyone had told me I should have first moved to, the queer-friendly one that was like a little city in and of itself. I lived across the street from a dive bar that had karaoke seven nights a week. I would go after work or class every day and get wasted and sing through the new thickness testosterone had brought upon my vocal cords.

The ground floor of my apartment building hosted three businesses: a barber shop, a driving school, and a Santería shop. That first day, while I waited for the realtor, I walked into the Santería shop. I've always been a spiritual dilettante. Having rejected Catholicism at an early age, I have always loved reading about the world's religions, trying to see myself fitting into them. Despite going deeply into Buddhism as a young person in New York City, despite almost converting to Judaism for my ex and her very religious family, I never found one that stuck. I walked into the Santería shop knowing a little bit about the religion from an ex from Cuba who practiced it.

The first thing I noticed was the replica Jobu in the window: the cigar-smoking, rum-drinking statue from the '80s film *Major League*. Jobu was a made-up deity in the film, the idol of a Voodoo practitioner who believed that appropriate sacrifices to Jobu could make him hit a curve ball. To say that this didn't exactly inspire my faith that this was a legit Santería store would be an understatement, but I walked in, anyway. I was in Cleveland, where tactless record stores put Black Lives Matter signs in front of cutouts of local celebrity Screamin' Jay Hawkins. Cleveland, if nothing else, has a sense of humor about itself.

The guy behind the counter was white—another thing that made me pause. It's not that I don't believe there are white practitioners of Santería with African roots, it's that I don't believe white people without them have a right to the syncretized religions that enslaved Africans were forced to create from their own beliefs and their captors'. It's like wearing a headdress or burning white sage: those practices are closed to outsiders who don't understand their necessity. If I felt differently, I would've started practicing Candomblé or Santería years before. But I did not want something stolen, something "exotic" that I could wow my unknowing friends with. I wanted something that I could claim as my own, something steeped in who I was as a person. I'd spent years reading about transness as parts of spirituality around the globe, and yet the closest I came to finding something that fit still didn't: the *feminiello* of Italy. In Italy, these transgender women (transgender here being a catch-all and probably not how they would describe themselves) are seen as lucky, and babies are often brought to them shortly after birth for their special blessings. This was the nearest I could find to something I could call my own, and it still wasn't my experience. For that, I would have to keep searching.

Still, I found myself suspending my disbelief and standing at the counter telling the man who worked there that I was looking for something to help my ex, the one who was a Santería devotee, who I hadn't spoken to in a few years, and who was very sick the last time I spoke to him. His orisha was Shango. The man led me to a red and black candle with a white outline of axes and lightning bolts on it. Then, probably to upsell me in the terminally empty store, he suggested I not light the Shango candle without lighting one for Ogun, who would protect me from the harsh demands of Shango. I took both candles.

I told him I was looking for tarot cards, and for protection. I bought a gilt-edged set of cards that never once gave me a proper reading (in fairness, I never blessed them, either). I bought a St. Jude medal, the patron saint of lost causes, and pinned it inside my leather motorcycle jacket.

I walked out of the shop. I would end up taking the apartment upstairs, despite all the imperfections I still couldn't see. When I would lay in bed at night, I could smell the incense burning from the Santería shop. It was probably all bullshit, white guy nonsense of pretending to be something he wasn't. But when I lit the Shango candle, I lit the Ogun candle. I lit a candle that my witch friend Gabby had made for me: it had herbs and a picture of Baphomet on it. She had promised me that it would bring me all my desires. I pulled tarot cards. I kept pulling the Devil, gilt-edged and sinister, all the time.

WAKING UP IN THE NIGHT

It is early 2021. I wake up at 3 a.m. I have woken up at this time of night every night for about four years.

It is still dark and will be for hours. I have recently gotten sober, started a vegan diet. But I am not eating more than once a day these days. I feel hollow and depressed all the time. My cat died in October of 2020, and my apartment is empty except for me. I have lived here for three years. The Santería shop has come and gone. The kitchen is a disaster, mainly because I do not have hot water in the sink and boiling water to do dishes is more effort than I can make most days. In the back room, a walk-in closet I have turned into an office, the ceiling is falling in. Every time there is another heavy rainstorm, chunks of it end up on the floor. There is black mold growing around the remaining parts of the ceiling and roof. Every time it falls in, the maintenance people from the building fix it with plaster, and it holds until the next rain. I wake up choking on post-nasal drip and sneezing from the black mold several times a night. Maybe this is why I keep waking up at 3 a.m.

In the main room, which serves as a living room and a bedroom, there are windows missing. They have been missing since November, when a tree with no roots in the back yard came crashing through them, narrowly missing me as I lay in my bed directly next to the windows. The day the tree came through the window, I heard a noise coming closer. Fear lightning bolted through me, disrupting my internal gray placidity, and I rolled instinctively from the bed to the floor. The tree branch shattered the window and landed in my bed. It could easily have killed me. The unconcerned landlord covered over the broken window with thin plasterboard and brought me a space heater to make up the difference in temperature caused by it. The winter wind cuts through the gaps at the edges of the plasterboard.

■

On a reputable health site, I find multiple reasons for waking up at 3 a.m.: stress, insomnia, sleep apnea, depression, drinking alcohol before bed. Any of these could apply to me, but something feels off about them all. On a sketchy blog, I read that the real reason for waking up at this time is unconscious or unresolved anger. On a Chinese medicine site, I read that this is the peak hour for liver activity, and waking up at this time means something is wrong in that area of the body. I wade back into the questionable personal blogs of self-proclaimed spiritual experts. Some believe that waking up at 3 a.m. is a sign of spiritual battle. Some believe it is the time of the Devil, as it is the time of night when Jesus died on the cross. The Catholic Church forbade activity from 3 to 4 a.m., at one point, believing it was the "witching hour." Yet others believe that waking up at this time means your consciousness is awakening.

■

I sit up in bed at 3 a.m. and pull my coffee table, which serves as an altar, near the bed. It is covered in a poppy-print scarf, candles, stones, offering cups. I take out my tarot deck, the Starman one created by an artist who worked with David Bowie his whole life, gifted to me by my literary agent when I was in a burst of work on a book of interconnected stories where fine dining servers in SoHo in the year 2000 are guided towards their dreams by different Bowie stage characters. I have been reading my cards every day, taking notes, trying to puzzle out my life with them. I ask questions and set intentions: How do I become a good person instead of just a good artist? What's the path to change? What do I do about my anger? How do I move to my radiant potential? No deck I've ever used before has spoken to me like this one. I have only had such good readings from other people.

In March of 2020, at the beginning of the pandemic, the writer Jeanne Thornton gave me a reading over Zoom. What I remember most of her reading is that she said my future would be defined by a written correspondence, and that the outcome card was Judgment, which she described as meaning Final Judgment, when everything that one knows burns up and is replaced by something new. In the last few days, Judgment has been the center card of my spreads over and over, the direct situation I'm in. The written correspondence—an essay I wrote about rape—has already been written and published and defined a lot of my life. Other cards tell me to focus on centering myself and warn me that I am in danger of burning out with a youthful brashness, dying young. When the cards tell me this, I stop drinking and taking benzos.

I remember the last day I drank. There wasn't anything dramatic about it: not like the time I woke up on a sidewalk in a rough neighborhood in Brooklyn, or walked those same Brooklyn streets drunkenly looking for heroin, or passed out on the floor at a party attended by kids I'd taught as a teaching assistant in grad school. No, that day, I walked into the bar I went to every day, looked around, and realized I was pouring my entire life into people I would never see again once I stopped going to the bar. How much effort I gave random strangers on a barstool near me, while the people who had loved me my whole life got none. I sat, had one drink, left quietly, and didn't go back.

But after stopping my drinking, the depression set in. I find it hard to stay awake all day. I lay in bed, napping, not reading, not going on the internet. I think about my life in the most negative terms. Everything beautiful or bright in the world around me has become shades of gray by increasing degrees. I send long, apologetic texts to the people who love me, describing myself as a black hole of need, saying how sorry I am that no one's love has ever seemed enough to me, how I am trying, really trying, to fill the bottomless hole inside me with the love that people have been banging their heads on walls trying to give me my whole life.

Every morning, I get up and read my cards. I write down the placement and the meaning and what meaning I derive from it as connected to my life in my journal. I light candles. I light a black one for protection and to ward off black magic, something I have feared a little since someone who I was sleeping with, who assaulted me, told me he often performs black magic spells on people he used to be involved with. To counter its possibility, at first, I tried to burn his name in a cup next to a card I drew at random from another gifted tarot deck, the New Wave Tarot. The card I pulled was Judgment, and the figure in the deck that stood for it looked scarily like me, with my all-black clothes and bleached blond hair. My rapist's name wouldn't burn all the way. The day when I burn the black candle with a mix of herbs blended into it, with the intention of protecting myself and my loved ones from black magic, my best friend's husband, who has been sick and going through a lot, goes to bed with a splitting headache and has a dream that a giant black centipede crawls out of the back of his skull.

∎

My depression started when I was a teenager. At first, talking about it felt like I was performing it, making statements that rattled around in my head, like, "Humans are just these strange beings, with wet holes that disease gets in, who all die." I wasn't sure I even believed it when I said it.

I lost my mind for the first time a few months later. I took acid and went to a show in a thunderstorm on top of a mountain, then drove to the seashore with my friends. At the shore, still hazy from the LSD, I walked down the beach and thought I knew the answers to life. They evaporated when a concerned woman, seeing my listless stare and wandering stride, asked if I was lost. *How ironic,* I thought. *Just when I had figured everything out.* When I went home, I laid in my bed in my mother's house and thought of a story I heard about how LSD makes the user's brain bleed. I was sure that my brain was bleeding, that if I fell asleep, I would never wake up. I wandered back and forth to the kitchen, carrying a gallon of orange juice with me, convinced the vitamin C would help. I laid in the bathtub, crying. My mother, not knowing what to do, took me to the local rapid health clinic, who said I had an ear infection from swimming in the ocean—swimmer's ear. I did not believe them, and it would be days before I stopped the flow of thought in my head that I mistook for blood from my brain.

I didn't understand what had happened. It would be a few years before these episodes became constant. It was after my father died, after my first boyfriend left me. I would experience what I now realize was depersonalization from depression and complex PTSD from a lifetime of hiding who I was. During those episodes, I would correct my journals from years before, forget I'd done it, think someone had broken into my house and crossed things out, written new words. I'd wander around deep Brooklyn in my Superman underwear and nothing else, my head and heart in states of overwhelming confusion. I was in and out of hospitals for years, misdiagnosed with bipolar I, then schizoaffective disorder, then bipolar II. I knew it was wrong, but when I tried not to take my unhelpful medications, I was taken to court to remove my right to refuse medication, labeled as a danger to myself and others. Years later, a therapist will tell me that bipolar medication, when misapplied to trauma, often makes extreme emotional states even worse. It is no surprise to me.

In the last ten years, since I came out as transgender, the depersonalization episodes stopped. A therapist, before I was hospitalized for the last episode, did emergency hypnotherapy on me, and combined with the cognitive behavioral therapy they taught at the hospital I was in, I began to trace back to the beginnings of the trauma-holes I often fell into in my brain. The panic attacks that happened every time I tried to cook meat? Related to that time when I was very small and my dad cooked pot roast, which my mother thought was undercooked pork roast and threw across the house at him, screaming that he was trying to poison and kill his children. My inexplicable fear of sharks in swimming pools? Related to that time my father threw a heavy plastic toy Jaws at my sister's face while we were in our swimming pool. Once I began to find the cause of these deep panics I faced, they began to lose their power. I began to see myself as a recovering survivor of trauma.

But the depression has never really abated. When it's at its worst, I cannot get out of bed. I have stopped starving myself and depriving myself of water during these times, which has helped stop the depersonalization episodes. Something in me has shifted where I no longer believe I don't deserve to survive, where I no longer believe I am like a rabid animal who needs to be put down, whose chances at life are all gone. I realize now how I would never think of any human this way, and I deserve the care I would show others, the belief in my own ability to heal.

■

I wake up in the middle of the night, at 3 a.m. It is dark around me.

I have long hung onto a belief, for around a decade now, since I first came out and became aware of the concept, that trans people in many cultures are marked as specially spiritually blessed, and that white people's colonialism and the damaging forces of Christianity tried to destroy them. That transness is a great inner trial that, once walked through, means the individual thereafter walks through the world with a special vision not many share. My depression and my trauma both inform my empathy for the world around me. I know for a fact that I see this world as few others do, that I have parted veils that not everyone has a chance to see beyond. In its most simplistic form, I do not view gender as immutable. I do not view binaries as solid. I do not view otherness as bad. I have deep empathy for all lives on the margins of what is considered normal and default.

But it has only been recently that I have begun to view myself, for my own sense of sanity, as a warrior going through spiritual trials. I have made it through so many. And, when viewing myself this way, it is easier to be easy on myself when not in the midst of them. It is easier to feed myself good food, to reduce the amount of drugs and alcohol I put into my body, to bathe in oils and treat my body well, to drink water and smoke less, to meditate and make connections to my spirituality, and care for myself. I think of my bouts of depression as battles. The world is not a safe or soft place for people like me, I understand this every time I walk down the street and am harassed, every time I turn on the news and see another politician attempting to set in motion the restriction of people like me from public life. I am a warrior fighting a battle against ignorance, against bigotry, against hate. I have lost so much in this battle: my family, many friends, anything resembling a "normal" life. And so, I must be my own comfort. I must build a little altar next to my bed and read my tarot cards every morning. I must put essential oils on my pressure points and feel their calming effects, or their invigorating ones. I must be kind and gentle with myself because there will be another battle coming soon, and I need to rest and rejuvenate between them. The wars will be endless, and one day, maybe sooner rather than later, I will not have the strength to fight them anymore. But while I do, I must care for myself in the lulls. I must make my bed soft and my connection to whatever spirituality I can find firm.

This is what it means to fight back.

This is not all though. I am not some saint that is spiritual and blessed. I can be a terror—lashing out viciously at people who hurt me, wanting to do anything to make the pain stop. My anger is electric and sprays out around me, injuring those who love me and those who don't. I cannot feel my body when it happens. I cannot sense that my pupils have dilated, my heart is beating faster, my fight-or-flight has kicked in. Around the time I realized I was raped the most recent time, I also realized how out-of-body I become in these episodes. When I try to stop myself from being vicious, people push me further, and the dam breaks, anyway, no matter how I've been trying to hold the water back. I say the worst things, the things that I know will hurt people. And later, I am always sorry.

Still, I don't know how to stop losing myself in this anger. My emotions are a tidal wave I cannot help but be subsumed by. The best I can do, the best I have ever done, is numb them away.

■

All my life, I have believed that art is the only way for me to speak to magic. I have believed in divine communication, muses, spirits, all of it reaching through human vessels to make beauty and terror in the world. I have believed this so hard and so long it has saved my life numerous times. One day when I was at an author's talk in my master of fine arts program, the poet CAConrad spoke about searching through the Edgar Cayce archives to see what the spirits think of poetry. The spirits, Cayce said, by way of Conrad, don't care about humans at all. They only care about making us proper vessels. I have spent my life in pursuit of being this kind of vessel, and my life has, in many ways, fallen apart. I remember walking through a mental hospital in my twenties, full of drugs, in a haze, writing down the images flitting across my head, working them until they became a story, even while I couldn't eat, speak to others, sleep. I carried my pages from place to place, writing until my mind became too unfocused to do it, resting, doing it again. In this way, my life has always been an evolving story. I write, I repeat myself, the details become clearer. I fully believe what Conrad found in those archives.

But recently, I have decided that this cannot be my only magic. I have struggled with addiction my whole life, struggled to come out of the closet as a trans person, lost family, struggled with finding a spirituality that didn't damage me. These days, as my depression is dark and overwhelming, I read my tarot cards every day. I don't know where to go with my spiritual quest. I order candles in different colors with herbs in their wax on Etsy. I struggle to remember stories of queer saints. I consult my witchy friends and light the candles they make for me. I try to piece together some kind of paganism that makes sense for me. It makes more sense than the religion I was raised in, which excluded the person I am.

■

Finally, I move out of the apartment without windows, with the crumbling ceiling, without hot water. I hope the waking up in the night will stop. It doesn't.

I move into a better apartment in a part of Lakewood called "Birdtown" for the streets named after birds, and for three days I nest, hanging art on the walls, buying the furniture I need for the new space. I feel like I will heal, maybe I am healed. I feel like I can face things again with less anger, as a better person.

Slowly, the feeling of being cracked open and empathetic to the world fades. I get calloused and numb, I go back to living in the world. I start drinking again, just here and there, enjoying it. I feel safe in my new apartment where there are no neighbors that I can hear beating their wives through the thin walls. I don't go to bars, and I don't take drugs. I don't feel safe doing that. But I sit on my porch and drink every single day.

One day shortly after I move, I see a post on my former MFA program's Facebook page promoting a play that is being directed by a friend of the person who assaulted me. The assault happened on this man's couch. The person who is in charge of the school's social media knows this, because I told her. I have never understood what a trigger means like I understand it in that moment.

I am livid. I am shaking. I am crying. I am full of rage and revenge.

At first, when I processed the assault, I believed the person who did it was not truly a bad person who had intended to hurt me. I believed he could be and do better if he faced what he had done. He would not face it. I am an anarchist and I believe that solutions have to come from communities rather than from a broken legal system. It turned out the community around both of us was just as broken.

The day I see the post, I reach out to a man who once helped me out with some legal trouble when I was an activist, who has become a friend, and who gives the best rational advice. I cry on the phone. I say I have done everything I can to stick to my convictions and none of it has worked. He agrees that I have, but tells me that no matter how perfectly I may stick to my anarchist ideals, it doesn't make an anarchist world around me. I talk about revenge, and he assures me that if I go down that path, I will be the one who ends up in jail. He quotes Mike Tyson: "Everybody has a plan until they get punched in the mouth." I say something I say often: all the cishet white boys are anarchists until they are worried about getting their asses beaten. He makes me laugh and talks me down.

My friend Vivien Zooms with me. We drink tea, hers a vanilla rooibos blend, mine unsweetened iced tea out of a plastic bottle that I consume with my cigarettes. She talks me down. She has just sent me a set of wrenches to work on my Vespa with, she says. She thinks it will be good for me to learn how.

The rage passes. The shaking stops. I feel as hollow as a canyon with the wind tearing over it. I don't know how I'm going to do any of this, ever.

■

A long time ago, people used to be very straightforward in their victim blaming of those who had been raped: What were you wearing? Did you say "no" explicitly? Did you enjoy it? People know better now, people are more subtle. At precisely the time I began to speak out about the fact that I had been raped, "friends" of mine (who were also friends with my rapist, who went to strip clubs with him, who joked that they would never leave him alone in a room with their girlfriends, who had him MC their lit readings) began to act as a jury about all my actions. That time I was drunk months before and got in an argument with a young poet, saying really cruel things to him? That was what this was about. The fact that I lash out when I'm angry? That was what this was really about. Suddenly, everything I had done months prior, which no one had discussed with me at the time, or ever really, was on trial. They said again and again that it had nothing to do with the fact that I was speaking out against their friend, my rapist, but it all happened at precisely the same time. I was no longer welcome in writing community settings. I was no longer invited to do readings. Friends who I had spent every day with stopped returning my phone calls. The rape, they insisted, was something else, between me and my rapist. They sent me emails I had sent to my rapist to prove that I was lying about it, though, too. "This you?" they said with the screenshots, like the Twitter meme. Despite that, they claimed that their suddenly judging me so harshly was something else entirely. The fact that my life was suddenly on trial by everyone who had known me and the man who raped me, that I was suddenly completely socially ostracized, had nothing to do with the rape, they all insisted over and over. And yet, there I was, scrutinized in every way.

Did you like it?

∎

I wake up at 3 a.m. It is dark. I go into my office.

I have been painting pictures using Nabokov's synesthetic color representations of letters. The idea, for some time, has been to "fix" *Lolita*, to preserve what people often claim is the letter-to-letter beauty of the text by removing all the words and only leaving these colors. I believe Nabokov was often painting because of this synesthesia when he was writing. I think of the soft, often pastel colors he saw, and how hard it must have been to turn them into such cruel words. I cut out paragraphs of the novel, cut the predator words out, paste what is left onto the canvases where I do these terrible, unskilled paintings. I do this in the middle of the night while everyone else sleeps.

It is like listening to sad music when you're sad. It's like hearing every word of a miserable song and evaluating it for how much it resonates with your own pain. I move scissors along the words carefully, leaving only meaningless phrases. I write other words in color.

It would be so nice to cut all this pain out from my reality, replace it with bursts of pastel, and so I do so on paper.

■

(In this blank space, cut out words that trigger you in this story and make something with the rest.)

■

On a Wednesday, I drive to Pennsylvania to get my first vaccine shot, because PA considers smoking a complication for COVID worthy of early vaccination, whereas Ohio does not. When I am in a Motel 6 in Youngstown, OH, on my way across the nearby state border to Hermitage, PA, I decide I'll stop in Akron and drive to my rapist's mother's house and tell her that her son is a rapist. I run it by my friend Vivien, who tells me I should call instead. I look her number up on one of those shitty personal information sites.

"Are you . . . ?" I ask, saying her first name and her son's last name.

"I used to be," she laughs. I know she is divorced.

I ask if my rapist is her son.

"Yesssss," she hedges. I think of times he has been thrown out of his mother's house for public drunkenness. I think about how he has told me his first memory is her telling him she will murder him. I don't care about the latter, not now. I am furious. All my empathy is gone.

"In 2019, your son drugged and raped me," I say.

She gasps and hangs up.

I post about the call on the internet. My best friend, Sarah, calls me to ask if I'm okay. I yell at her. She reminds me of when I said people aren't disposable, that we should do our best for them. She says she doesn't give a fuck about this guy but cares that I am doing alright. She says it sounds like I am processing.

"If I have to face consequences for speaking out about this, so does he," I say.

I walk around outside the Motel 6 while we talk on the phone. There is a man hosing down the windows. There is a couple yelling in their car.

We get off the phone and I go back inside. I go to the pharmacy to get my vaccine and come back. The vaccine hasn't made me feel the slightest bit of discomfort, so I decide to go visit my friends Bill and Rebecca and their two kids, who all live in Youngstown. Bill used to be friends with my rapist but isn't anymore. Bill believed me when many, many people who were friends with my rapist did not. I drive over to their house in my rental car and we take their kids to the park, where they show off and point out the graffiti that's repeated around town and that their dad wrote into a short story about time travel. I feel safe. I feel comfortable, and calm.

When I get back to the motel, I fall asleep early. I wake up at 3 a.m.

■

I think, often, that trauma never ends. You learn to deal and cope with it, but you never know what will put you back to square one. You never know what is lurking somewhere innocuous, waiting to rekindle all the feelings that you thought you had done the work to get over. You never know what's going to take you, one day, from someone quietly enjoying the life they've built since the trauma, to someone who is full of murderous rage. Progress, in so many ways, seems like it should be linear. But it's not, not with trauma.

I am better, I tell people and myself. I will do better.

But I'm not, and honestly, why should I be? Why should I be a victim who goes about things acceptably? Why should I not feel rage and anger? My body will not let go of the trauma, and I am expected by so many to move on, to get over it, to go on with my life. And yet, when I see a reminder of my trauma, I am reacting worse than I imagine I did in the moment of it, or even the next day, or even the next year. My body is releasing tears, my body is shaking, time no longer exists. A whole day goes by. If I can lose this time, any time, if I can be reduced to nothing but a body that has been harmed and how it reacts, how can I move on?

I am broken, and I have tried so hard to fix myself. I have taken my pills, prescribed. I have taken other pills, unprescribed, but which I feel are necessary. I have drunk myself stupid. I have tried therapy. I have tried meditation. I have thought about revenge. I have thought about suicide.

None of it is better. Nothing is better. I am not better. The person who did this to me will keep doing it, as he's been doing it for years. There is no changing anything: the past, the present, the future.

■

When I woke up naked the next day, went home, and saw the blood coming from my body, I thought, somewhere in my head, *It's not like this hasn't happened before. Get dressed. Go to school. Go to work. Go on.*

■

I cannot be hurt, I thought, then, and for years before it, *if I accept the hurt. If I seek out situations where I know I am not cared for, not loved, not treated with respect. Because then I will not be blindsided by it.*

My mind believes this lie for a long time. My body does not. My body remembers and stores that memory until my mind can face it, too.

■

After the morning I woke up bleeding, he made me cum so many times. He used his hands to make me orgasm again and again. I still think about these orgasms, even now, even after everything.

■

I wake up at 11:30 p.m. I wake up at 1 a.m. I wake up at 3 a.m. I cannot stop crying.

■

When I move into my new apartment, and am decorating, I put together a collage in an empty frame I have for the wall of my office. I put a card in it that was given to me at the launch of one of my books, at a small and tasteful bookstore in east Cleveland. My rapist, who was there, signed it, along with everyone else. My eyes move to his signature. Above it, it says, "Remember the moon." A few months before, when a poet was visiting my MFA program, the person who raped me sat in on the craft talk the poet gave. He asked, "Did the moon landing change the project of poetry?" The room was full of stifled giggles, but I think it was a good question.

I'm also reminded of one of the albums that the man who raped me and I both adore: Leonard Cohen's *Songs of Love and Hate*. In "Sing Another Song, Boys," Cohen tells of a disastrous affair. He reminds us, before the song begins, that this is an old, bitter story, one he would like to be rid of singing about. The man in the song, lying in a heap, standing where it is steep with conviction no one has ever been where he is before, self-important in a ridiculous way, reminds me a lot of the man who raped me. Cohen says of the two lovers in the song, "Ah, they'll never, they'll never ever reach the moon / At least not the one that we're after / It's floating broken on the open sea, look out there, my friends / And it carries no survivors."

If I have to feel this pain, everyone around me will feel it, too. There will be no survivors.

■

I pull a tarot card from my deck. It is inverted. An Earth Queen disconnected from the Earth.

■

In May of 2019, a few weeks after my rapist gave me drugs and fucked me when I could barely stand, I sat in my bathroom with a belt around my neck that I intended to attach to the shower rod and hang myself with. I didn't know, at that point, I had been raped. It sounds odd to say—who wouldn't know when they had woken up naked and bleeding with no concept of how they had gotten that way? My trauma is lifelong, and when new traumas come up, I do not react to them immediately. I told myself it was fine. I was a fuck-up. Things like this happen in my life every now and then. The belt around my neck, in my mind, had nothing to do with the assault. I couldn't find a rational reason for it. It was the month before I was to launch a book I'd worked on tirelessly for six years, which was finally being released by a powerhouse indie press I'd interned with in my twenties. I was going on a book tour from New York City through the Midwest in June, something I'd dreamed of all my life. My future looked bright, but I could think of nothing but this endless, nagging pain I was in. I couldn't stop drinking. I couldn't think of anything but any possible way out of the pain.

Right before I attached my belt to the bar in my shower, I texted a group chat I was in to say that I was about to hurt myself, that I needed to check myself into the hospital, and I needed someone to care for my cat while I was there.

It had been eight years, at that point, since I had been hospitalized. When I got to the hospital, a doctor told me I'd been misdiagnosed for the last twenty years—that I had complex PTSD, not bipolar disorder.

I didn't know what I was doing there. I got out. In June, I left for book tour. In Minneapolis, I sat on a park bench with a decades-old friend and told him how I was killing myself with drugs and alcohol and I wanted to stop but didn't know how. I had no idea that more trauma had been compounded on top of what was already there, had been there for longer than I could remember.

■

No one has ever hit me quite like my rapist did: open handed, his arm drawn back far, the contact of his hand with my face abrupt and stinging. This was how he always hit me, whenever we had sexual contact. The night he raped me I only remember in flashes, and most of them are these blows to my face. When I woke up, my body from the neck up and the waist down was screaming in pain.

■

There are times when I have dreams about my rapist. Many nights. Most nights. Sometimes I wake up sweating, on my back, my hips locked tilting up and my body painful.

■

I said earlier I no longer believe I deserve to die. But sometimes I still do.

■

My rapist has used the words over and over, "You wanted it."
    While this is a standard rapist phrase, there is some truth to it.

When he offered me the drugs I took that night, I wanted them. I took two pills. I asked him to put another one on my tongue in his car. I took a fourth at his friend's house.

I did want the drugs.

He says I wanted to fuck him that night. I cannot tell you what the case there was, because I have no memory of the night after all the drugs he gave me. I know I never wanted to sleep with him before that night. It's also worth noting that, other than that night, I've never seen him do anything but cocaine. But that night, he bought pills, my drug of choice. I don't know if he took any or not.

He says I wanted it when he hit me during our sexual experiences together after that night. It's true that I like being slapped and choked during sex. It's also true that every time we engaged in rough sex, I had to stop him and explain the difference between liking rough sex and wanting to be hit so hard I bled. There was never any discussion of boundaries, there were never any safe words, there was never any aftercare. Almost every time we had sex, I woke up groggy and bleeding from some part of my body the next day.

There is a fine line, which isn't really a fine line at all. But some of it, I did want. I also did not want him to do things the way he did. I had to tell him over and over that he was actually just hurting me.

■

I drink a smoothie and decide to lay off the alcohol again. This lasts a few days.

I navigate conversations with friends after one of my rapist's friends, who I also thought was my friend, tells everyone that I'm a violent bully and they shouldn't speak to me anymore. I explain my behaviors. I get mean when I feel attacked and need to make the attack stop: a PTSD reaction. I had asked my rapist's friend if he could get me opiates, something he is now saying was a microaggression based on his race. My rapist's friend and I had been doing drugs together for two years, and after I relapsed on my rapist's drugs the night he raped me, the game was back on with no limits. I asked his friend because he always had access to drugs, something I knew from doing drugs with him multiple times. If you don't want an addict to ask you to help score them drugs, I said, the simple solution seemed, to me, to be to not give them drugs in the first place. I explain that I didn't rape my rapist, despite what he's told everyone, that I'm physically incapable of what he is accusing me of when he says I dragged him into the back of my car and forced his hand into my vagina. I explain myself over and over; it is taking up all my energy. A former friend who I called out online says he has a panic attack over it, and suddenly I am a bully again for pointing out that it's a lot easier to virtue signal your support for rape survivors who you don't know in the larger writing community, while talking shit about rape survivors in the community around you and going to strip clubs with their rapists.

I start drinking again. Every day and night, I drink. Every night, I wake up around 3 a.m.

■

I start talking to a trauma therapist from a free therapy clinic nearby. I am in one of my good periods, a lull between triggers and overwhelming emotional storms. She tells me over and over that I sound like I'm doing great, that I'm doing her job for her, and I probably don't need therapy. In talk therapy, I often cheat by planning out what I'll say beforehand, engaging my strong intellect while neglecting my feelings. She buys it. She never asks a single question about my emotions, which are often more than I can deal with, which I have always been willing to do anything to shut off and ignore. She doesn't understand my radical positions on police or community and tells me that she thinks rapists belong in prison, that my rapist engaged in all the standard rapist behaviors, from drugs to emotional manipulation, and maybe I should go to the police. Just after I relapse on alcohol and tell her so, she texts me to say that she forgot to tell me she's going to be out indefinitely for a planned surgery. I can text, she says. She sends a hug emoji, which I think is highly unprofessional. She does not set me up with any other options for counseling. Two days later, with no therapist or potential therapy in place, I face a massive trigger, and am back where I started. I am drunk on whiskey. I am snorting the number of benzos a friend took in a suicide attempt, just so I don't have to feel anything.

THE THINGS WE CAN'T TELL OURSELVES

(Use this blank space to face something you cannot face.)

The things we can't tell ourselves, we still know.

In May of 2019, I am sitting on the dirty floor in my tiny bathroom wondering if the shower curtain rod will hold my weight.

The pain has come back—I don't know why, not now. Everything should be fine. I have just published a memoir and my novel is coming out in a few weeks. Everything should be great. But all I can think of is how much pain I am in, how oppressive it is, how it will never go away, how suicide is probably the best option.

I text a friend to say I'm suicidal. She says she's suicidal, too. I don't know what to do. I don't know who to reach out to. I text a group chat I'm in, asking someone to please take care of my cat, because if I don't go to the hospital, I am sure I will hurt myself. Before I go to the hospital, I draw a tarot card. The Seven of Cups. Temptation. Being overwhelmed. This is the deck of tarot cards I bought at the Santería store downstairs from me. It is gilt-edged, and it never gives me good readings. But today it is on the money.

In the ER, they give me a pill, and I sleep like a newborn for sixteen hours. Somewhere in my drug twilight, they have me speak to a crisis counselor. I don't remember what I say to her, but she decides that hospitalization is the best option.

There is a moment that's happened to me often, though not in a few years. I am in the back of an ambulance, watching a city recede behind me as I am driven off to a country hospital, strapped down to a gurney. It always feels vaguely like I'm being thrown out.

■

At 8 a.m., on my ward, a woman yells, "Jesus wants you to believe!"

"Jesus wants you to be quiet!" someone else yells back.

"What are you?" the first woman, Sharon, asks at my door a few minutes later.

"Go away," I reply. She does.

When I come out of my room, she says, "I thought you were a boy when they brought you in. I'm glad you're a girl."

I go back to my room.

■

I pace up and down the halls. I sing Bruce Springsteen until I realize that I've sung the word "suicide" several times and stop.

A phlebotomist tells me that Sharon has been in the hospital her whole life. She was in the children's ward. Now she is gray-haired, and still here. In my early twenties, nurses warned me against being the kind of person who was in and out of psych wards their whole life.

There is a Bible in the hospital. I read the book of Luke. I am struck by Luke's retelling of Jesus's words instructing people to love their enemies. I have heard this before, but never past those three words. Jesus says that even the evil love their friends, but to love those who have wronged you is his way.

I think about being a better person, extending kindness to everyone, but the second I am informed that the nurse in the ER never took my keys to give to my friend so she could feed my cat, I curse, "That motherfucker."

■

When I am in the ER, I tell them that my main problems are drinking and being off my HRT. They say the deciding factor in where I will go will be my health insurance. They send me somewhere that doesn't treat alcoholism or prescribe HRT.

■

"She still dances on marble legs for the king of the ward," Sharon says. I think about schizophrenia, and how many poets I know would kill for this natural convolution of language.

I think about Lucia Joyce, James Joyce's daughter. She was a dancer, schizophrenic. She and Joyce spoke in a secret language, allegedly the basis for *Finnegans Wake*. Beckett pretended to love her to get closer to her father. She was destroyed when she realized the ruse.

She spent most of her life in a sanitarium. The Joyce family guards her as a secret, crushing most attempts to write about or discuss her.

There is a well-known picture of Lucia Joyce before her hospitalization. She is dancing, wearing a flapper dress, bent back at her waist. She looks like a picture of demonic possession.

I think of this poor girl, the time-honored role of mad muse for mediocre men. What we can't tell ourselves, we still know.

∎

"Wonderful, wonderful Jesus Christ the cop killer!" Sharon wanders through the halls yelling.

I pace them. It takes three minutes for a full circuit. I wonder what it would be like to have these halls, the courtyard, be your whole world. Sharon picks weeds from the flowerbeds in the courtyard every spring.

∎

The medical doctor lists all the systems of the body that alcohol damages. I have just woken up, am cranky and defiant, sitting on his examination table.

"I know," I say.

He does not give any suggestions on how to stop drinking, or how to fill the moments it fills.

The doctor asks, "Do you ever wish you could go to sleep and not wake up?"

I don't know how to tell him I wish it all the time, almost every day, have wished it for decades, so I just say, "Yes."

■

Xan comes to visit. She is quiet, thoughtful, beautiful, with a streak of sarcasm that occurs like lightning bolts through her regular peacefulness. She brings me chips and chocolate.

"People keep asking me," I say, "why I'm here when I have so much going for me." The psychiatrist asked this when I told her about my writing career. The police officer who took my possessions asked me this when she saw my books.

"No one who loves you thinks that," Xan assures me. "We just want you to get better."

■

"We know you think you know what your problems are," the psychologist says, "but we have to treat your suicidal ideation."

"You say you have to travel on Monday," an aide at the front desk says when I'm told my departure might be delayed until then.

"What, I'm making up my book tour?" I ask.

"I don't know. Maybe," she replies.

"You sound like a fucking idiot when you open your mouth," I tell her.

They don't change my medications. They don't offer me therapy. They offer rooms where people play Mad Libs with Tupac lyrics. They offer stickers and marble notebooks. No one gets better. I don't get better. I'm not even sure what I'm trying to get better from.

A TAXONOMY OF MAGICAL THINGS

CANDLES

Black for protection, white for purity, red for love, pink for self-love, orange for courage, yellow for clarity, green for money, blue for healing. Some of them have herbs embedded in their wax. Some, you carve with sigils and words and names. Some you anoint with a protective oil you made. All of them, you burn. You unfocus your eyes and see the aura around the flame, and you imagine it growing bigger and bigger until it seeps out of your bedroom, out through your kitchen, out your front door, over your lawn, over the train tracks across the street, down the Cuyahoga River, into the glassy expanse of Lake Erie, and through the world, carrying your intention with it. You put them in a little hand-painted bowl you ordered from Morocco, and you burn them until their wax puddles run together at the bottom of the bowl, harden, become impossible to remove. When the wicks get low, you are burning all of your intentions, all at once.

TAROT CARDS

Four decks.

The Illuminated Tarot is the gilt-edged and -inlaid one you bought at the Santería shop downstairs. It is beautiful, and flashy, and it never, ever works for you or anyone you read for. Sometimes you draw just one card, and it is so often The Devil—addiction, submission, being beholden to that which will destroy you.

The Starman deck was a gift from your agent. Tarot are supposedly best gifted, and this tarot works best for you. But when you start reading other people's cards with it, it is so difficult. It just wants you. You begin to bless it thoroughly each time you use it, lighting palo santo and waving it under each card.

The Modern Witch Tarot was a gift from your former friend Dani. Dani lived across the hall from you in your last apartment in Cleveland until she bought a house with her partner and moved out. The deck reads well for you, simple and easy. It is a modern, diverse take on the Rider-Waite deck. The last time you spoke to Dani she had moved out of your building, and you were furious with her, as a job she brought you into, and then used you as a reference to get out of, had forced you to work while ill, and then forced you out after you were hospitalized. She refuses to talk to you about what you are going through, and your mean side comes out, telling her about the times she's fucked up in your friendship, been inconsiderate, and what a user you think she is. You never speak again. When fall comes that year, you haul all of the garbage she left in the backyard out to the curb. The deck—it's a really good deck, though.

The New Wave Tarot was a gift from your friend Michael. He sent it in a care package with books, the cards, pins for your leather motorcycle jacket, and, inexplicably, PEZ dispensers. Michael is an older gay writer who you respect a lot, whose work you adore.

You think of him as an old gay uncle—to be fair, you are always adopting older men as your uncle-figures. The Judgment card in this deck, when you bleach your hair blond, looks just like you. One day, when you tell Michael about a binding spell you did, he will tell you that when he does them, he puts pictures of the people he's binding in a box lined with mirrors and throws it in a body of water, cursing them to forever be haunted by their own selves.

MATTRESSES

There are two in your apartment: a cheap foam mattress from Walmart on a cheap folding bedframe, and a cheap black futon mattress covered in your cat's hair. Your rapist has slept on both of these mattresses on drunken nights, and sometimes your skin crawls, thinking that you are sleeping in his hair, flakes of his skin. It is only when you move away, when you get rid of these mattresses and sleep on a friend's in their spare room for a month, that you stop having nightmares.

HERBS

In little bags, at first, tucked onto a shelf in your kitchen: mug wort, rue, lavender, cloves, organic cinnamon sticks, black salt, yarrow. As time goes on, as you collect more, you will buy little glass jars wherever you see them—the Family Dollar, Target, wherever—and label them and put these herbs in them. You will also grow basil on your windowsill, and stock your cooking spice cabinet with parsley, bay leaf, sea salt, black peppercorns. Each has its purpose, and while you don't remember them all, you know some by heart. Rue, a bitter herb which can kill in large amounts, and which offers protection. Yarrow, one of the oldest healing herbs. Sea salt, to cleanse, and black salt to intensify any spell.

RECIPE BOOK

Ever since you began cooking professionally, you've been stealing recipes and writing them in a little purple Moleskine hardback notebook. At first you just remixed the recipes you had taken from others, making them you own, but eventually you began to create recipes that were all yours. The book, now falling apart and stained, has all of these, plus drawings of plated desserts, vegan recipes. One day, when you were walking down the street with your chef friend Jake and his sous chef, Paul, Paul offered to carry your bookbag.

"Run for it!" Jake instructed him as he took it from you.

You laughed. "There's nothing in it but some books, my notebook, oh, and my recipe book."

"I mean it, run!" Jake laughed as Paul took off down the street.

SPELL BOOK

You began this much like your recipe book: by writing down other people's spells. Then, as time went on, you took your own notes, created your own potions and ways of casting. It's not as big or as full as your recipe book, but it is something you think you will give to your niece one day, with the little purple recipe book as well.

PLANTS

Basil you planted on the Equinox.

Also:

Your first plant that survives is a gift from your friend Christina, who is also the person who initiated you into witchcraft. The initiation ceremony was in your backyard and involved rose petals and spoiled wine. An unsuspecting 7-Eleven delivery man, laden down with cheap but drinkable wine, walked into your backyard in the middle of it, while three of you were screaming in laughter, singing "Put It in Your Mouth." You still have the piece of paper that Christina wrote the date on in the inside pocket of your leather motorcycle jacket. There are rose petals wrapped inside it. It's under the pinned medal of St. Jude, the patron saint of lost causes.

The plant Christina gave you was a small succulent in a tiny pot that read "YOU ARE LOVED ALL THE TIME." It was two inches tall when they gave it to you. Now it stands at six inches. It has outgrown the pot that reminds you that you are loved all the time. It reminds you itself, in its quiet voice.

The second plant was given to you by your former friend, Dani, who was also at the initiation ceremony. You don't know what kind of plant it is, just that she named it Martha, which happens to be the name of one of your favorite Tom Waits songs. Your friendship is over, but the plant still thrives, spilling out of its pot, hanging down the windowsill it sits on. It reminds you, in its quiet voice, that we keep love even when it ends.

MARDI GRAS BEADS

These are the beads that your rapist's girlfriend put on your neck the night that he fucked you in the back of your car. Later, when he says you assaulted her that night, that you assaulted him, you will remember her putting these beads around your neck when you asked if you could kiss her at the dive bar across the street from your house. They lay coiled around the radiator in your bathroom like a snake. You never clean your bathroom. That's why you never threw them away.

HANDKERCHIEF

You can't remember when your rapist left this behind. Was it the night that he stepped on your silver boots and took it out, got down on his knees, and wiped your shoe off at the bar while everyone laughed? Was it the night that he fucked you in your car while his girlfriend slept on your futon mattress (are her skin and hair in that mattress, too?)? You keep it in a drawer with your socks, underwear, and silk pocket squares. One day you tell him you have it, and he says he would like it back, but you do not give it back.

LITTLE STATUES OF THE BUDDHA

You keep these on your altar. There is no particular reason. You are not a Buddhist. But they were given to you years ago by your first boyfriend's brother. You have kept them, carried them, never lost them, for over twenty years, and you are not going to lose them now. The Buddha is sitting cross-legged, his hand raised, and a bowl in his lap.

ESSENTIAL OILS

You put them on to energize yourself (mint, tea tree) or to calm yourself (lavender) or, that one time when you are sitting at the taco place with you friend and their friend says your root chakra is blocked, you go home and anoint it with orange oil and try to sing from deep down in your diaphragm to unblock it.

TAROT CARD HOLDER

A little wooden crescent moon with a space for a tea light candle and a notch where you can prop up a tarot card so it stands upright. The point is to meditate on that card all day. When you buy *Around the Tarot in 78 Days* and each days holds meditations and exercises, you dutifully prop up each day's tarot in the notch.

GREETING CARD

It is signed by everyone who was at the book launch for your memoir, including your rapist. You let it haunt you for a long time, his faux-poetic words above his signature, "Remember the moon."

MORTAR AND PESTLE

A small, marble one you purchased on Amazon because the ones in the witchcraft store were very overpriced. You don't have much use for it, so a small one will do. Occasionally, you grind herbs in it.

HAIR

Though hair is used in many spells (along with blood, spit, and fingernails), there is no particular reason you save the rattail with the last wisps of blond at the end of it that you cut off your head just before you interview for the job that will get you out of Cleveland forever. There is no particular reason, but you put it on your altar because you like the way it looks.

A MOVING LOCUS

There was a woman in my rehab who had smoked a lot of PCP. PCP, incidentally, was first developed as an anesthetic, but came into street use not only for its numbing of pain, but its hallucinatory properties. PCP also makes its users irrationally violent and aggressive at times. PCP is a drug that the man who raped me once went on a long diatribe about wanting to use via text message to me—how it was maligned, how it wasn't as bad as everyone thought it was, how much he wanted to try it. These text messages were deleted from the ones his lawyer sent to my lawyer after he sued me for writing about the rape.

But the woman in rehab—she is who I'm talking about. She was an older Black woman with several kids. She would start talking about "him." Sometimes she meant God. Sometimes she meant the Devil. Sometimes she meant her ex-boyfriend. It was always wild to hear her dive right into a diatribe about "him," and wade through it with her, trying to figure out which of these figures she was railing against.

I kind of liked following this moving locus.

■

It's fall when I start going to rehab. All summer long, I drank hard with my friends in my backyard, or sitting alone on my porch, or snorted so many Valium I blacked out entirely. But summer is ending, and fall is nearing, then it is there. I hang up dollar store wraiths with glowing eyes and long gauze trailing behind them on my porch, I put up fake gravestones with ominous warnings in the lawn, I paste little vinyl bats all over the rails and walls of the porch. I have never done this before, decorated my house for anything. I have never had a front porch, either, mostly living in apartment buildings and foregoing holiday cheer.

But this year is different. This year, I feel something in the cooling air. I have started to go to a pagan AA meeting at a local witchcraft shop. We sit around and talk about readings from the pagan version of the AA Big Book. After one of these readings, I go stand in my backyard, in the falling rain, watching the wind move the leaves on the trees. I, as suggested in the early pages of Pagans in Recovery's Big Book, try to see if I can stop nature, make the leaves swirl the way I want, make the wind blow the way I want, make the rain fall in patterns I choose. I cannot. The tree leaves swirl of their own accord, the rain comes down without heeding my requests. Something—something holy, something unseen, something deep in the mechanisms of nature—is doing the things I cannot. I stand near the spot that used to be a firepit, which is now overgrown with invasive plants, where, earlier in the year, my friend Christina initiated me into magic with spoiled wine and rose petals. I try to stop the rain. I am powerless, but there is a power there that I cannot change or fully understand— the first step. The world around me is preparing for hibernation. The leaves are dying. The air is growing colder. My old neighbor, Dani, has left so much garbage behind in our yard. I drag it all to the garbage bins when I am done standing there, marveling at the things I cannot change. Cleaning up a mess is one thing I can.

■

My friend who has a healthy prescription for Valium and Adderall started giving me large amounts of the former when I was stressed out about an STI that someone (probably my rapist) had given me. They would give me twentysome at a time. The days after they would give them to me are a blank in my memory. I would snort one, not feel much, snort another, feel a little, and keep snorting until everything was flashes of reality. I would go about my life, going to a writing workshop my friends held on Zoom, going to friends' birthday parties and potlucks. Then, several days later, I would wake up trying to piece it all back together. This started the night I was raped, when the only reason I knew for sure I had been was that I woke up completely naked with the person who had raped me sleeping on the floor next to me. After that night, I wanted oblivion. I didn't know why, I just knew that I didn't want to think, see, feel—not anymore. It's notoriously hard to overdose on benzos, but I did my best, drinking hard while I snorted them. Later, a friend who is in the medical field will tell me that whiskey and Valium is "an instant heart stopper." I never ended up in the hospital, though, just woke up trying to piece the previous few days together from brief glints of memory.

■

(Use this blank space to piece together a time you blocked out with drugs or subconsciously.)

The structure of trauma can be slippery. It moves when you think you have a finger on it. It rises up when you think you've successfully pinned it down. It asserts itself in waves that crash over your unsuspecting head when you think you are swimming along just fine.

This moving locus is not one I'm particularly fond of. It occurs to me that this is probably the same motion the woman in rehab follows when she talks about "him."

■

Sometimes, a lot of times, I'd look for drugs on Grindr. One day, after I started rehab, but before I really got sober or thought I necessarily had to, I found a guy who was selling Adderall. I bought a bunch from him while he picked at his feet on his couch. He told me he was attracted to trans men, and he'd gladly give me Adderall if I sucked him off next time. I said I'd think about it but, in reality, was offended he thought I'd suck him off for such a cheap drug. He texted me over and over after that, and I ignored him every time.

That night, I snorted a bunch of the pills with my friends Paul and Amanda. When they left, I had around twenty-five Valium in a vial. Two days later, all the Valium were gone, and I wondered what I had been doing. People told me they had talked to me in the days that were gone from my mind. I didn't remember any such thing.

It is difficult to write about your life when so much of the years you are talking about are a blank. When things have happened, when you've done things, that cannot be pinned down entirely. I am telling the truth, and yet—there are so many holes in the fabric of my memory. Here, as I write, I am attempting to weave this torn fabric back together. I wonder, as I write this, what all victims of traumas wonder: *Will I be believed?*

■

The woman who smoked PCP seemed to be holding it together somehow. She had smoked so much of it, but the horror stories that I often heard about people who had taken a lot of that drug either didn't apply to her, or she had learned to mask their side effects. The only place you could see the effects of the drug in her were her speeches on "him."

"I just want him gone," she would say, and then she would launch into a long speech about the effects he had on her life. We would all listen until, finally, the woman leading the session would say, "Who?"

"That man, that evil man."

It could have been her boyfriend. It might have been the Devil. We would only know if she told us.

■

One day, after rehab is over, when it is winter, and I've successfully straightened out my life a bit, my friend brings over Suboxone. It is the kind that comes in a sublingual tab. I put it under my tongue and let it dissolve. It tastes awful, medicinal and lingering. Within a few hours, I'm puking, nodding off, falling asleep. It feels just like heroin, but it's designed so that you can't overdose on it. It feels like coming home.

I have a phone appointment with my therapist from rehab shortly after that. She calls and I cry. I hate my job as a pastry chef at a university on the East Side. I hate the commute, I hate the awful weather we're having, snow that I wade a mile through to get to the train that takes me to work, then half a mile through once I get there. Nothing seems like it will get better. And I took Suboxone.

"Well, I got high in a harm-reduction fashion," I tell her. "The person I got high with is someone who would never hurt me, and I took a drug you can't overdose on."

"This sounds like you're making excuses," she says.

I get mad. I am talking about how I am doing my best, making better choices than I had in the past, even if they're only better by a little bit. I hang up, still mad. A few days later, I tell my friend who gave me the Suboxone about the conversation.

"It does sound like you're making excuses," he says.

And maybe I am. The focal point of my sobriety—its necessity, and my adherence to it—is something that is often in motion.

■

On Halloween, I got to an AA meeting at the local pagan shop. I take a bus across the suburb I live in and wait outside. In a mirrored surface, I think I see someone in a cloak approaching from my right, but when I look around me, the person is coming from my left.

After the meeting, I buy some herbs. I buy lavender, mugwort, cloves, cinnamon, and nutmeg. They are too expensive for herbs, but until I stock my kitchen the way I want to, they will do. I am making a potion for Samhain, the night when the veil is thinnest between the living and the dead. The purpose of most of the herbs is to keep me safe and to give me clarity, though I throw the lavender in for love. I don't know why I do. Love has always terrified me with its limerence and lack of clear-sightedness. Love has always harmed me more than anything else. But I buy the lavender anyway, hoping the herbs for clarity help me overcome my predilection for seeing just the sleight of hand.

I go home, boil them all in a pot, and drink it down.

■

Women reach out to me in the months after I come forward about the rape, before I go to rehab. They talk about the person who raped me holding them down when they were drunk, trying to have sex with them, them fighting him off. They talk about him pushing them down in neighbors' lawns and trying to have sex with them after walking home with them when they'd both been drinking. They talk about him exposing himself to them.

They all want to talk to me about this to tell me I am not alone. But when I find out he is suing me, when I find out I will have to face him in court, none of them want to talk about it anymore. It is too scary, the thought of having to look him in the eye in a courtroom and repeat what he has done. I agree because I am terrified to do it, too.

And, so, I am alone again.

■

One day my upstairs neighbor tells me that the dollar store wraiths I hung on my porch blew upwards in the wind, coming to the front of his balcony rail, scaring the shit out of him.

"I guess they're working at keeping the spirits away," he says.

■

I buy little glass jars, and I put my dried herbs and flowers from the pagan shop in them. I label them all. I line them up on my shelf so that none will be mistaken for another. Sometimes, I take the lavender out and smoke it over tobacco, which in many European witchcrafts is used to banish negative things or people.

There is a degree of order that I never had in my life. Everything has its place; everything is accounted for. I look around at the disaster of my existence and wish for this kind of clarity.

AN ELEMENT OF SURPRISE

Every night in 2021, I go on Grindr. Grindr in Cleveland is full of DL men who would fuck me but never admit to it if asked. I represent "man lite" to them—someone they can fuck to fulfill their desires of fucking a dude without actually thinking of me as a man.

The person who raped me—despite having sex with me, a nonbinary trans masculine person multiple times—considers himself straight. I think of the violence of these interactions, the same violence I know he has used against multiple women I'm acquainted with. It is always a surprise to me that gender, our relationship to it, and how it plays out in the world is dependent on so many factors of the world around us. We can only be what is reflected back at us. In New York City, I was firmly transgender, moved mostly amongst a circle of fellow trans people. Here in Ohio, my gender is mutable, indistinct—I am who people will make me with their desires, their hatred, their prejudices, their fear. Moreover, I am who I am made by my own fear of those who have caused the most harm in my life. Then there is the layer of sexual assault, of being public about it—does this negate my "maleness"? Does my transition negate my role as a survivor? It depends on who you ask.

After the assault, I lose count of the men I fuck. I fuck a guy in his twenties who's home from college. I fuck a guy who, when

I later find out his last name and Google him, turns out to have stabbed someone in a Steak 'n Shake parking lot at 3 a.m. a few years ago. I fuck a guy who says he's into me but acts like an asshole the next time I have him in my house. I fuck a guy who puts a leash around my neck and makes me walk to his bedroom on my knees. I fuck a woman who straddles my face and suffocates me with her cunt. I go out on a few dates with another woman, who I never have sex with, who is wealthy and who I think of letting take me away to another country to live with her.

I don't know what I'm looking for, except to get off. Or maybe I do. Maybe I am looking for someone who will hurt me—not the way my rapist did, and not without boundaries—but someone who will understand what kink and casual sex and queerness are in the way just about everyone I knew in New York did. Someone who will choke me without attacking me and making my neck sore for three days after. Someone who will slap me, but not like they're angry with me. Someone who will call me a slut or a cumhole, then hold me afterwards because it was just a turn on for both of us, not how they really thought of me.

I don't find these things. Not in Cleveland. I find casual sex that means careless sex. I find people who want to cum in me but don't ask my name, who disappear off of Grindr the next day. I find people who I am less than human to. And this is what I start to think I deserve.

It hasn't always been this way.

■

It's spring, I'm twenty-nine, and the woman who will later become my wife but who has, now, just recently become my girlfriend, has broken up with me for the first time. I am a wreck. I find myself on FetLife, the fetish dating site that I barely use, looking for someone to fuck away my misery.

I find someone I have several people in common with, a burlesque performer named Dreadful Rick. Dreadful Rick is into dirty talk and wrestling and being fucked in the ass with strap-ons and bondage. When I get to his apartment, someone outside nods and smiles at me, knowingly.

He lives in Bushwick, his whole place is like a theater production, gossamer curtains of multicolored cloth hanging around, masks, paintings. Dreadful Rick is a high school teacher. He has a partner. He isn't looking for anything serious, and he's very busy with the other aspects of his life. We both understand this will be a onetime thing. We negotiate what we both want. I am scrawny, not out yet, still identifying as a cis woman. In a short time, we are throwing each other across the room, grappling, pinning one another down. I am not scared. There is nothing scary about clearly stated desire, people who check out across community lines. Dreadful Rick pins me down and makes me say his name.

■

It is a clear, bright Saturday in 2019, the early September sun directly at noontime prominence. I am walking back home from looking in on friends' cats while they are away, down a long street, over a set of railroad tracks, towards a main thoroughfare. I am singing along to my headphones. I hear barking as I walk, background noise, animals behind fences, behind closed doors, up on porches behind baby gates. I don't pay it any mind, walking, singing. Usually, when I walk, I carry pepper spray in my hand, but the day is bright, neighbors are out on their porches, all is well.

One dog's bark sounds more vicious, more urgent. I look up to see a pit bull spring off of the porch next to the part of the sidewalk I'm on. The dog rushes at me, and before I know it, he is biting and I am kicking and then I am bleeding and his owner is dragging him away and I'm screaming, "Why wasn't your dog on a fucking leash? Your dog took a chunk out of my arm!" My blood rivers down my elbow, onto the ground, it splatters onto my shoes and pants like a murder scene.

■

It's 2021, summer, around midnight. I ride my Vespa to the apartment of some guy who sent me pictures of himself on Grindr with hundred-dollar bills and drugs. He is cheesy, pathetic, I think—but he has drugs and that is what matters. I walk into the open door of his apartment.

He's on the couch with his pants unzipped, jerking off when I walk in. I don't say hello and neither does he. I get on my knees and give him head while he sits on the couch, watching something on the TV with the sound turned down low.

I finish, spit his cum out in the sink, and he hands me a bag of pills. I don't look them up, I just take them. I go home and take one. It's shitty ecstasy, clearly cut to hell. It makes me feel strung out like a meth high with hints of euphoria. I take two more.

It's the Fourth of July and I am supposed to have a party in my backyard. There are a handful of people coming over and I keep telling myself, from 1 a.m. onwards, that soon I will stop taking these shitty pills, that I will go take a nap. I never do. Christina comes over around 3 p.m. and makes me eat fast food because it's been around twenty-four hours since I've had food in my body, then takes me to the grocery store so we can buy food for the party. They grill and cook everything.

My friend Marzi is there. Ver dad has just passed away, and the only reason I still had the get together, even after all the drugs, was that I didn't want ver to be alone on the first holiday after ver dad died.

We sit in the yard with my friends and my AA-loving neighbor who always bums cigarettes off me. Before the sun even goes down, I excuse myself and go inside to sleep.

■

An attack has to have an element of surprise to mean anything, especially when you're transgender, especially when you've been through hell and trauma and loss and funerals and found your friends after they've tried to kill themselves. Some things you expect. I expect, for example, to be assaulted. But where it's coming from is sometimes a surprise

■

I laugh on the way to the ER after the dog attack, make jokes to the paramedic. I call my best friend and leave her a giggling voicemail. I am bandaged and alive, elated in the back of the ambulance. I can't think of the word for "first aid kit," and keep calling it an "emergency box."

This is shock.

■

Nothing bad can happen to little "cis" twentysomething me, in combat boots, with a shaved head and a pink triangle pin on my jacket. Not now, in New York City, where everyone I know knows everyone else. Community, even with people you sometimes hate, is a safety net in New York. Nobody wants to end up in a callout on Queer Exchange. You know where you are going and who you are with. I haven't been assaulted since I left the shitty town I grew up in, where men's sexual abuse was shrugged off with, "That's just how he treats women." It will be years before my wife proves me wrong, violates my sexual boundaries softly but violently, nonetheless. Little "cis" twentysomething me fucks Dreadful Rick, a stranger, whose house I am comfortable in, who I have wrestled with all morning despite his ability to hurt me with ease if he wanted to. Little "cis" twentysomething me slides a strap-on into his asshole while he moans, "Oh, daddy."

■

In the summer of 2020, a carful of young men passes me on the road. It is purple dusk, and I am wearing shorts that display my extremely coarse, thick leg hair. Overuse of my chest binder has bruised one of my ribs, so I am in a sports bra, my breasts much more visible than usual. The boys lean out the window screaming, "Learn to love Jesus or go to Hell!" at me.

Screaming from a car has an element of surprise to it, because there is nothing the person on the street can do to retaliate, and it is over as soon as it happens. The person on the street, if they were just walking home, if they weren't quite expecting it, if they had their headphones in singing along, is left staring after the car, wondering what to do.

■

I walk home from the ER with the flesh of my arm stapled together and bandaged, convinced I am fine. This is likely the Percocet talking, because when I fall asleep at 6 p.m. that evening, I wake up every hour, heart racing, breathing hard, having had a trauma nightmare that I am trying to close a door and a wild dog is pushing through it.

The next day, I walk to the grocery store to bring home everything I can carry in one arm. I don't notice a dog behind me until the last minute. It is leashed, docile, gentle, but I run and break down in tears.

I go home and call the ER I was in the day before begging for more Percocet. That isn't something they do, they say. They can hear the desperation in my voice, which I'm sure they've heard in the voices of many addicts. Crying, I ask what I am supposed to do about the pain, and they advise me to take Tylenol and try to sleep it off.

■

Danger can come from anywhere. On a sunny street, at dusk, from a man with a chipped tooth, from a dog, from a carful of boys, from a man at a bus stop, from someone you think you know.

■

Dreadful Rick wants to go down on me without a dental dam, bury his face in my unshaved, unwaxed pubic hair. I, back then before the invention of PrEP, always had strict rules about hookups, and my partner who just broke up with me and I were "fluid-bonded," a state where we only shared bodily fluids with each other, no matter how many other people we fucked, always using condoms and dental dams for everything. At first, I say no. We talk about risks, statistics.

■

Right after the dog attacks me, a man runs out of the house next door. He is carrying a first aid kit. Someone who I assume is his son calls an ambulance while he wraps my arm in gauze, elevates it above my head, promises me that if I am calm things will go much better. His pressure on the wound is gentle, his words soft. When the ambulance finally arrives, they look at the job the man has done and say how lucky I am he was there.

■

After I break down in the grocery store parking lot the day after the dog attack, I call my best friend, Sarah. I keep telling her about the guy who bandaged my arm in the street the day before. How I want to send him a card. How I want to thank him. "You know that Mr. Rogers thing, 'Look for the helpers.' It's true, that guy was who Mr. Rogers said to look for," I weep into the phone.

■

The guy who puts the leash around my neck and fucks me while we watch porn is from California, and he and I have communicated desires, wants, limits, and all the things we should have. This is still one of the hottest sexual experiences of my life.

■

The guy who gives me drugs that suck texts me again the next night, and I tell him he is a poser and his drugs are awful. He asks if I'll suck him off again.

■

I finally agree to let Dreadful Rick go down on me. It's not that I feel pressured into it. It's that I really want to feel his mouth on me, to feel freed from the fluid bonding to a person who doesn't care for me, who has discarded me, who will later take me back and break my heart even worse. So, I take the dental dam away and when his face is surrounded by my clouds of pubic hair, I feel released. He's gentle and skilled at what he's doing; I come again and again. It feels good to have someone help me reclaim myself.

■

There was a time when I was safe. In Ohio, that time is long over.

PART TWO

THE TOWER.

"While it may appear that some outside force strikes down the narrow-minded person, the violence shown on the card actually derives from psychological principles. The person who lives only to satisfy the ego demands of wealth, fame, and physical pleasure, ignoring both introspection and the spiritual beauty of the universe, raises a prison around himself. We see this prison in the Tower; grey, rockbound, with a gold crown. At the same time a pressure builds up inside the mind as the unconscious strains at its bonds. Dreams become disturbed, argument and depression more common, and if a person represses these manifestations as well, the unconscious will often find some way to explode."

—RACHEL POLLACK, *Seventy-Eight Degrees of Wisdom:*
A Tarot Journey to Self-Awareness

A BRIEF HISTORY OF ASSAULT

The first time I realized I'd been raped, I was twenty-six years old. I was sitting in a folding chair at a Take Back the Night rally on my college campus. Take Back the Night is a 501(c)(3) that, according to their website, has a mission "to end sexual assault, domestic violence, dating violence, sexual abuse, and all other forms of sexual violence" and "create safe communities and respectful relationships through awareness events and initiatives." When the microphone came to me, I remember talking about a man who I'd been involved with, and how the first night we had sex, I was passed out on the floor of his living room and woke up to him inside me. I remember saying, at the rally, that it "was my fault because I took the drugs."

■

I had been fucking a guy who was married, who first had sex with me when I was unconscious from booze and pills on the floor of his living room. The next time we had sex, he choked me into unconsciousness without my consent and had anal sex with me. I kept sleeping with him for about a year.

I had a mental breakdown shortly after that. I remember, in my psychosis, thinking he had broken into my apartment and edited everything I'd ever written.

Years later, when I send a copy of an essay where I am processing rape to another rapist, he sends me back an edited version. I think about his edits for a long time before letting them into my work. I write essays where both of our voices are in the text. I decided to be as kind as possible, to display how he must have felt, while still speaking my own truth. In a way, letting the person who raped me reconfigure my work was something that had long been in my head.

■

When I went away to college, I was able to see that this first incident was rape. It was still a long time before I saw it wasn't my fault. Christian-based AA had done a number on me, convinced me that everything that had gone wrong in my life, I was at least partially, if not entirely, to blame for. I was sober when I went to college, but not a healthy kind of sober: the kind where you are barely hanging on. In AA they refer to this state as "white-knuckling." I was severely mentally ill, but I hid the extent of it, for the most part, pretty well. About twice a year, I would have breakdowns that necessitated me being hospitalized.

I started hanging out with a group of student radicals while I was in college. Most of the people I spent time with went to different colleges around New York City, not my small undergrad near NYU. I loved them fiercely, in a way that I'll probably never love another group of people again. It was the kind of friendship you have in youth, where you all agree on the big things, where your group cohesion is both reflexive and desperately important. A lot of us were born in the month of September, and I remember the years when we'd have group birthday parties with dozens of people in whatever house we were throwing them in. The dissolution of that friend group is still one of the most painful memories of my life.

In the small university I did go to, there were a group of theory-heavy, asshole anarchist guys. They were respected by a lot of people, but not so much by others. One of them, a grad student, had been dating a young woman who was in undergrad with me. I didn't know either of them very well. What I do know is that at some point, she accused him of raping her. And that he and his theory-bro friends said it wasn't possible because they'd been dating. And that a group of her friends, clad in black and carrying baseball bats, went into his apartment and beat the fuck out of him.

He couldn't go to the police, obviously, not while keeping the respect of his anarchist friends. So he walked around campus for weeks, his face bruised and healing, everyone knowing what he had done, and what had been done to him in return.

■

I slept with one of that guy's friends twice, incidentally. The first time was fine. I think I bruised his ego when I laughed at him for trying to cuddle with me after, because the second time we slept together, he threw me out of his apartment as soon as he came. I never spoke to him again.

■

Years later, I was gay-married. I had a diaphragm fitted when I was dating a partner whose primary partner insisted that he use two forms of contraception every time he had sex outside of their relationship. My wife liked for me to use the diaphragm, but due to my body dysphoria centered on my vagina, I hated when she orgasmed inside me when I was using it. It meant I had to keep it inside me for twenty-four hours and then pull the spermicide-wet, slimy cap off of my cervix. One day, I asked her to wear a condom because of this discomfort, and she insisted that condoms made her dysphoric. Finally, I relented and put the diaphragm in on the condition that she not orgasm inside me. She did it anyway. After, she said, "I just basically raped you." I cried for two days and put it away in my head. I loved her. It was an accident, I told myself, even though I knew it wasn't. Even when I walked into a show of hers she thought I wouldn't be at, and she was in the middle of telling it as a funny story, the time she "went for it" without my consent. I put it away. I put it in the back of my head. I pushed my feelings down. Then, a year later, when she violated the boundaries of our relationship severely, this time by breaking our fluid bonding with another partner, we sat in my therapist's office, and without even thinking of why, I said, "This is worse than the time you raped me." My therapist looked stunned. My wife began stammering and eventually left the room.

A few months after we'd broken up, I did a radio program where I talked about our relationship. When it went live, her new girlfriend attacked the producers, attacked the show, and attacked me on Twitter. My ex-wife, though I'd used a pseudonym for her throughout, insisted she'd been deadnamed in it to this woman who was now screaming about it on the internet. Her new girlfriend finally calmed down and stopped. About four months later, she wrote me to apologize for what she'd done. My ex had sexually assaulted her, she said, multiple times. And she knew she couldn't speak up about it, not with how protected my ex was by her carefully chosen inner circle of people with relative power in their community. The woman was sorry for how she'd believed my ex-wife's narrative about how she'd been abused and discriminated against by me. Now she understood.

My ex-wife has written me several times since then, most notably when her sister committed suicide. She apologized, then, for how her family, who had never liked me, treated me. She did not say a word about her own behavior.

■

Besides the assault, besides her controlling nature that separated me from my friends, my ex-wife and I weren't always unhappy. We made dinner together. We rescued a cat from a construction site together. We made music together. There were plenty of times I loved her.

And still.

■

When I was living in Geneva, Ohio, I invited a man who called himself a "total top" over from Grindr. When we were having sex, and he was behind me, I reached back to find that his condom was not on. I let him finish. At the time, rapists were calling removing condoms in this way "stealthing."

I thought about dying a lot in the next few days when a cloak of depression fell over me. I didn't think about rape. It took a week to understand that this was wrong. That this should not have happened. That this was not my fault. It always takes me a while. Years later, when I'm in rehab, my counselor will say that the more I learn to care for myself, the shorter the time will be that I will stay in situations that disrespect me. This sounds great. I will think to myself that I cannot wait until I can see the wrong being done to me as it is done, not weeks, months, or years later.

■

I was in a hotel room in New York City, drinking vodka with a guy I'd met on Grindr, who had a chipped front tooth. He was fucking me from behind when I realized he'd taken the condom off.

■

The rape that happened in Cleveland, Ohio? Social ostracization, lawsuits, being told I was a liar who appropriated the language of others' lived experiences of pain. Sometimes I wish I never said a word about it. It was the time I chose to fight back. It was the time I learned how severely I would be punished for doing so.

■

And that guy—he hates me now, but it's impossible to tell this story without admitting that there was a time he didn't hate me, and I didn't hate him. We were friends, even.

■

I know I've forgotten some. That's how many times it's happened. I don't pretend to know much about signs, but when assault becomes a non-event, something that you can't always recall the details of, I don't think that's a good sign.

THE COLOR OF THE CAST

(Use this blank space to write a memory you are unsure of.)

When I was about seven years old, my father broke my older sister's arm. Or so I thought. I was there, watching. I saw the fight they had. I recall when my mother asked me what had happened after and I tried to defend my father, who never hit me, who I loved. I can still remember the green cast my sister wore on her arm that summer, which matched her lime-green polka-dot bathing suit. She wrapped the cast in a plastic bag to get into our above-ground swimming pool. I remember it down to the last detail.

"That never happened," my mother said dismissively, when I brought it up much later, when I was in my twenties. "You make things up. This is just one of your stories."

This was a common refrain throughout my childhood. I was precocious, writing novels since I was able to read them, spending hours pounding away on a manual typewriter I'd found at a yard sale. As a child, I did sometimes make up stories; a shadowy man lurking outside the next-door neighbor's house who I admitted was an invention when my father said he'd have to call and tell them there was an intruder, an invisible friend I was mimicking from reruns of some Nick at Nite sitcom with children. But whenever something was too hard for my mother to confront, to look at directly, she would deflect by telling me I had made it up, that I read too much for my own good. Childhood is a space of openness, of testing. Our parents should tell us there is not a ghost in the neighbor's yard, but they should not use this same policing of boundaries on the hard-to-talk-about.

I thought about my sister's cast throughout my youth. I remember my sister and my dad fighting. I do not remember him hitting her in such a way that might break her arm. But it was such a flurry of violence. I was so young. I remember her arm being broken. I knew at least that was true, despite my mother's claims.

My sister and I do not talk. This is understandable, as she spent her childhood suffering from physical abuse, and I was saved from it by my father moving out shortly after I was born (he spent a lot of time with me but left when he lost his temper). She is eleven years older than me, and even if she was the kind of person who could ever consider me anything but a little brat sent to annoy her (she's not), I suspect she's always hated me because our father never hit me like he hit her. She inflicted a lot of the violence inflicted on her back on me in my young years. But once, when she was visiting our mom's house in Pennsylvania from California, where she'd run off to the minute she was able, and I was visiting from New York City, where I'd run off to the minute I was able, I asked her about the summer her arm was broken.

"Did Dad do it?" I asked.

"No," she replied. "We were arguing, and I punched the wall because I was so pissed off at him. Me and Gram made up the story about it being his fault to make him feel bad."

It's enough to drive you crazy, to grow up in a family where even the always-fractured truth is broken into even more unfixable pieces. For a long time, it did drive me crazy. I spent my twenties in and out of mental hospitals. At one, I cried in the bathroom all night, sure my mother had died. When the doctor asked me how I could know such a thing, having spoken to no one since I'd been there, I asked him how you could know anything was true, ever.

■

I came out as transgender when I was nearly thirty years old, but I knew I was transgender when I was five. I was open about it when I was young, able to discuss that I did not feel like a girl at all. But the mind of a child is easily discounted, especially in the case of transgender children, even today.

The detractors of transness presenting in early childhood say, "How could they know what gender they are? Children think they're dinosaurs, they don't even know what they want for lunch."

Gender, as an experience, is something deeply personal. I could not tell you how I knew I wasn't female-identified at five, just that I did. It wasn't just about GI Joes and race cars instead of Barbies and baby dolls. It wasn't about baseball instead of cheerleading. When I would argue with my mom at the department store, convince her in my relentless child way to buy me underwear with superheroes and a front flap on it, it felt right. When I shopped in the boys' section, I saw the person I wanted to see in the mirror.

Around the same time, a gay coworker of my mom's was murdered, and suddenly my gender expression was no longer allowed. I understand it now as fear, but it's hard to look at how that fear came out in enforcement. My siblings policed my imagination games and drawings. "Mom," my brother would call, "she's pretending to be a boy again!" My sister would throw a fit about how embarrassing I was to the sympathetic audience of my mother when I didn't want to wear a shirt. I had previously gone around bare chested and free, somewhat tolerated for my eccentricity to that point.

As clearly as a child knows their own mind, their mind can be molded to believe the things they know of themselves are wrong and inexcusable. It's standard gaslighting, telling someone what they experience is not the truth, thereby making them question their own sanity. Gaslighting is often done by abusers to keep their victims in line. It's done to children—not just trans children—all the time. "I'm hungry," says a child. "You just ate, you can't be," says the parent. What you feel is not real, what you see is not there, what you are is incorrect. There is a direct connection to the culture of silence and violent "correction" of childhood my older sister experienced through physical abuse, and what I experienced as a trans child told they could not possibly be who they knew they were.

The effects of sustained gaslighting are often dramatic. Low self-esteem, depression, the inability to test one's reality. Psychosis is a more infrequent effect, but one I experienced all through my twenties. I walked through the world feeling that everyone knew more about me than I did. And in some ways, I was right. When I went to my first therapist, and he recommended I try a gender identity clinic, I was shocked. I couldn't be one of those people. Didn't he see the long hair I'd begun straightening and caring for in my twenties? The lip gloss boyfriends had told me made me look so much better? I was not what this therapist thought I was, I was convinced.

But I was. I always had been. I had been so effectively told I was not, that such a thing was then out of the realm of my constricted imagination.

■

Fairytales are part of childhood, and the absence of parents in them is what allows the fantastical events that befall the children in them to happen. Mothers are missing, fathers are dead, the children are left without guidance. There's also the wicked stepmother trope (see missing birth mother) that allows for and inspires many of the cruel fates in these tales.

There's a famous assumption about childhood and fairytales and psychology that says they are safe grounds for exploring terror because the terror is always somewhere outside. The terror is in the woods, or the haunted house, or the castle. The absent parents are something we don't worry about tucked into our safe childhood beds, being read the story by our mother, if we are lucky. The woods are dark and deep, but they are far away.

But what if the terror, even in our safe beds, is that which comes from those who are supposed to protect us? What if our parents are not absent, but convinced of another reality in which our fears and truths do not exist? What if we asked them to believe us and they said, *No*. What if they said, *You are crazy*. What if they said, *You are not the person you think you are.* What if you then walked through your life looking at people who, deep down, you knew you were like, obsessed over them, watching every film and reading every book with a trans character, fascinated, making mental leaps about these obsessions, your own nascent bisexuality, vague queer community connections, allyship, and support, while never being able to imagine yourself as one of them? Who you are is suddenly outside, what you once knew was true is the looming terror you cannot face, nor look away from.

■

It took me decades to undo the tangles of growing up in an abusive family who strove to keep a bright coat of paint on our white picket fence. It took me years to recover from the trauma of being raised by a transphobic family. The combination of the two were disastrous. My family is mostly shipwrecked and separated. I do not speak to any of these people anymore for my own sanity. There is only so much you can take of your reality being questioned and disregarded.

I wonder how many other people my age have experienced this. Not just the ones from abusive families, either. Even my lifelong best friend, who was raised by a loving, accepting mom and dad, would worry that if she saw a ghost, she would have to live with it as a fact of reality that no one else could accept. That she would have to walk through life facing horror that no one else thought was real.

"Would you believe me?" she would ask, over and over.

There is a certain terror in that.

The terror is greater, however, when you have become convinced that that which is solid and real is the ghost you invented. When you can remember the color of the cast, but you cannot remember, for twenty-five years, who you once knew you were.

■

I can remember the time of childhood testing when I knew the difference between fact and fiction, no matter what my mother tried to tell me, no matter what I raved in mental hospitals. For a time, between the combination of drug use and what's only recently been diagnosed as complex PTSD from extended childhood abuse, fantasy and reality grew fuzzy in my mind, collapsed under the weight of what I was told, who I was made to be. It was only when I was nearly thirty years old that I stopped being paranoid about the things I was hiding from myself, began to parcel out fact and fiction into easily identifiable categories.

BULL'S-EYE

It is the end of 2018. I have applied for and failed to get a grant to stay in a motel within driving distance of Centralia, PA so I can work on my master's thesis, a multigenerational, slipstream, experimental novel set in the coal fields and haunted places of the mining valley I grew up in. I have not been approved for any of the grants, prizes, or fellowships associated with my graduate program since, in my first semester, I objected to one where students were publicly pitted against each other before winners were decided. It was gross, I said in my letter of rejection to the people who had nominated me, to take a cohort of artists and teach them that competition was more important than mutual support. It didn't surprise me when I didn't get the grant for my thesis research.

But a friend has a wedding I'm going home for on New Year's Eve, and I can make the trip double as research. My friend Mia gets on a bus in New York, and I start a backroads drive from Cleveland, OH, to Wilkes-Barre, PA. My car is an old-new SUV that will never make a trip this long again—in fact, before 2019 is over, it will be repossessed because I'm unable to pay the predatory loan I took out to get it.

Mia and I meet at the bus station, and I take her to Tommy's

Pizza in Kingston. Tommy's Pizza serves deep-fried Sicilian pizza, a local specialty that I've never found anywhere else but where I grew up. Mia is a tall, gorgeous trans woman: she wears plastic cat-eye glasses, has a fierce streak of gray in her short-cut hair, and an effortless style. She transitioned when she was very young, much younger than my nearly-thirty age of transition. I spent several awkward years from age twenty-nine to thirty-three or so struggling through potential style, buying the standard-issue patterned short sleeve button downs and bow ties many trans-masculine people wear. While we sit in the booth of Tommy's, me with my beard and bound breasts, I think of how little I pass, here at home, and how I hope I don't see anyone I know.

A few days before the wedding, Mia and I trek to Nanticoke where a series of old concrete buildings that used to house mining personnel still stand in the woods. It's a lost city, the Appalachian coal mining valley's answer to storied ruins. It's only a short walk into the woods, but it feels miles from civilization. I have not been to these ruins, called Concrete City, in decades. We wander through the snow and climb the crumbling stairs that wind around the corners of the insides of what is left of the buildings. Black soot from the fire department trainings that now happen in the ruins stains our gloves and coats as we use the dirty walls to keep our balance.

We are walking through the trees when Mia sees a rolled-up poster attached to one of them.

"What's that?" she asks.

Excited, we both walk towards it and unroll it.

It is a bull's-eye with bullet holes all over it.

We look at each other. We are thinking the same thoughts of being alone, readably transgender, out in the woods in Trump country.

We let the poster roll back on itself loudly as we run towards the car.

■

Something has changed. I am no longer comfortable in places I once was. Perhaps the middle of the Pennsylvania woods was never a safe place for a young woman, but I spent most of my childhood and teen years there without much of a feeling of danger. The middle of the Pennsylvania woods is definitely not a safe place for an openly and visibly transgender person.

But it isn't just the woods.

The first year I was at my master's program in Cleveland, OH, shortly after moving to the state from New York City, I was one of the "stars" of the program. I sold two books my first semester, both to respected independent presses. I worked for the university press, where we often went out to dinners with visiting writers. I was nominated in my first semester for a fellowship at a writers' summer program with tuition and lodging paid by the school (this is the one I withdrew my application from). I tend to move into things wearing rose-colored glasses. Before I joined my MFA program, a favorite professor of mine from undergrad who had written my letter of recommendation said that he would of course write a recommendation, but that I might want to evaluate the program to see if it would be worth my time. The capstone, 150 pages of fiction, was something I'd done before I'd graduated from my liberal arts undergrad college in New York, eventually pub-lishing the work as a novel. I ignored the warning.

The glow of having been accepted and welcomed to a master's program in the arts wore off before the first year was over. The sleight-of-hand became more apparent, just like it had the first time my ceiling fell in from the rain in my apartment. Sometime in 2018, months before my trip to Concrete City, I had become uneasy with how a fellow trans student in the program was treated at our graduate assistantship placement. She ended up having a mental health crisis before my second semester was up. It was around this time that I learned about the student I'd replaced in the graduate assistant placement: a young Black man who was fired because taking care of his family came before his work at the university press. I was growing more and more uncomfortable as I looked around me.

In good standing with the people who ran the placement, I thought, I decided to speak to my supervisor about it. The conversation started with me bringing up concerns about how the other trans student in the placement was being treated, moved into me making suggestions for accommodations a trans person with a long history of trauma might need, and veered towards my cisgender, white, straight female supervisor spitting, "You don't need to explain inclusion to me," continuing with her trying to convince me I would never find another job at the school and would be forced to drop out of the program if I didn't like it there. It ended in the school library with her yelling, "Was I not funny enough? Did I not make enough jokes?" at me as if we were in the middle of a horrible breakup. It's funny, now. At the moment, I was mortified. I quit my graduate assistant placement before the semester ended.

Almost overnight, I was a pariah to my master's program's faculty. I tried to understand what had happened. I had been outspoken in undergrad, organizing with radical student groups, disrupting classes, agitating for recognition of students who, like me, could come nowhere close to affording the quarter million dollar four-year tuition. I had still been well-regarded by almost all of my professors, friends with my fellow students. There was the obvious difference: I was attending a public university in Ohio where students lobbied for guns on campus in the midst of nationwide school shootings versus the progressive, private liberal arts college I'd attended in New York. There was the fact that as a white, queer student in undergrad, most of the professors who took me under their wing were people of color and queer folks who firmly understood what it was like to be a minority in academia, whereas the English department I was now in was largely the whitest, most cisgender, and heterosexual environment I'd ever seen. Those were obvious.

But there was also the fact that I had changed. When I navigated the world as a white queer "cis" woman, I was offered respect. I was viewed as "assertive," and "confident," and "tough," all desirable qualities. As a white transgender nonbinary person, I am often called things like "too political," "aggressive," and "standoffish." I am the same person. The world has begun to view me differently than before.

■

Mia and I are wandering through the abandoned city of Centralia. In preparation for this part of our trip, I look as female as I can, now that my identification is distinctly no longer female. I shave my face. I don't bind my chest. It's a level of protection.

Mia, as long as I have known her, has never been one to be clocked aggressively. Her SoCal accent lilts and drawls over a voice that's higher in register than mine; she's tall, skinny, and beautiful. She looks like a stunning queer model. There is no getting around that both of us will be read as queer by anyone who sees us.

We walk around what's left of the town that was abandoned when a relentless mine fire started under it in the '60s. It wasn't vacated right away: people got sick and died, holding onto their homes as the noxious fumes rose from the ground. All that's left as we wander through it in 2018 is a church, a cemetery, a municipal building, and two houses. We look at the hulks of abandoned fire trucks inside the glass doors of the municipal building. We wander through the cemetery. We pass the houses, peeking in the windows. They look, inside, like someone will be right back.

Up on a hill, Mia points to a plume of smoke coming from another hill. "What's that?"

"That's the mines still burning."

We cover our mouths with our scarves.

The book I am writing is a ghost story, at heart. A family that is haunted for generations by spirits, and, in a near future, holograms of those who are dead but not quite gone. When I was a teenager, I stomped around the valley I grew up in in combat boots, dreaming of writing about the place I was born. I hadn't seen enough of the world, didn't know anything back then. Now, in my thirties, with two books on the way, I am finally getting to it.

We wander through the abandoned city until we are so hungry we have to leave. On the way back, we stop at a pizza shop, the only place we can find open in the lull between Christmas and New Year's that we're in the middle of. A rough-looking cishet couple gets out of a truck and walks inside while we are eating. They are the only other people in the cramped space. I eye them warily.

Mia, who is far more personable than me, starts talking to them. They learn we were just in Centralia and begin to enthusiastically show us pictures on their phones of all the abandoned ruins they've been to recently.

I breathe out a sigh of relief. They are fine. We are fine.

■

When Mia and I are driving back to Wilkes-Barre from Centralia, we see signs for Hazelton, where my father was born and raised. It is also where he is buried. I mention to her that I haven't ever been to his grave other than on the day of his interment.

"Do you want to go now?" she asks.

"No."

We decide to stop in Hazelton, anyway, to get the tires of my car looked at, as I think I can smell rubber burning from the passenger seat while Mia is driving. While we look around for an open mechanic's shop, I see the pizza place my dad grew up with, that he loved more than any other local pizza. I see the cemetery far in the distance.

"Are you sure you don't want to go?" she asks.

"No," I say again.

But we don't go. The mechanic tells us my car is fine, and we get back on the road.

◼

In graduate school, the microaggressions pile up. The eyerolls from my former supervisors at program events. The comments from other students. The absolutely problematic things older white women write for class. The straight-up aggression. I find myself in the middle of controversy after controversy inside class and outside of it.

Sometimes I look at the people around me and think, "It must be me." My peers, fellow students who I love, keep me sane; they are also shocked at the behavior of some of our professors and classmates.

One day I walk through the English department's offices. There is a glass case there with everything anyone connected to the program has published in book form. There is even the undergrad literary magazine. At this point, several of my books are out, one is a finalist for the state's longest-running writing award—a fact that was ignored when the department announced the university press's books that were finalists for the same prize. None of my books are in the case.

◼

After my friend's wedding, after Mia goes back to New York, after our trips to all the haunted places I can think of around my hometown, I start to drive back to Ohio. I drive through the backroads of eastern, then central PA. It begins to snow when I'm a few hours from Wilkes-Barre, and I stop to stay at a hotel right next to "Pennsylvania's Grand Canyon." A younger, different me would have walked along the edge, even climbed over the guardrail to get a better view. The me that exists now remembers the target on the tree that Mia and I so slowly unrolled. I stay in my hotel room, writing, until it is time to drive home.

IT WAS RAPE

*(Use this blank space to write about a
violence you do not remember.)*

My adjustment to the Midwest was not an easy one. I moved there from New York City after a traumatic divorce. Cleveland, before I moved there, had seemed like a place that could hardly exist for me, despite the fact that my best friend since childhood lived in a nearby town. I couldn't fathom the Great Lakes, in a lousy lived-in-NYC-most-of-my-life way. The thought of leaving my queer, sex-positive community in New York for some ghostly industrial city in the middle of the country wasn't something I ever thought would happen, until it did. I found myself living on the East Side, attending a master's in fine arts program at a group of public universities. Within the first year, I hated the consortium program I was in, hated half my professors, hated a good portion of my classmates who considered me "too political" in my decidedly trans, anarchist writing style.

I was in a poetry class a year and a half into my master's program. A close friend and I had taken it because there was nothing else open and we needed the credits. The class was a ridiculous one about what the professor called "literary capers," taught by an old white man with a '70s ponytail who thought his old white man friend's book of poems where he posed as a Hiroshima survivor was an appropriate thing to teach in 2019. It was not a surprise, given this environment, and also utterly a surprise, when a fellow student took out a piece of paper during her workshop time and delivered a manifesto to the class about how alienated she felt as a cishet white woman, how other minorities were given more consideration than her. It was decidedly racist and transphobic. She singled out demographics. She made a long speech about not understanding pronouns like "they," which I use. After she finished, after the professor nodded and moved along with the lesson without comment, I stood up, made a scene, yelling about how she had called out fellow students by identity, making her as uncomfortable as she'd made me. My friend and I left the class midway through. We drove back to Cleveland from the Kent

State campus, where the class had been, marveling at what had happened, unable to really believe it. My friend dropped me off at a bar near my house where several other people we knew from the local lit scene were hanging out.

One of these people was a guy named <<redacted>>. I had met <<redacted>> several times before then, because, despite the fact that he'd graduated years before, he still went to all the parties, readings, and dinners that the program held. I did not like <<redacted>> when I first met him, and that he was close friends with someone who had been accused of raping his girlfriend didn't sit well with me either. <<Redacted>> seemed to like me, though—was always starting conversations with me about the concerts we'd both been at, about sadboy music, about writing. I was trying to keep it together that day after the incident in class, get drunk and be fun to hang out with, while I explained what had happened to the group of guys who I was now hanging out with. Before long, everyone but me and <<redacted>> was gone from the bar. I was drinking hard, whiskey on the rocks, my usual. At one point, when we were very drunk, <<redacted>> leaned over to me and said, "I've been wanting to ask you—you matched with me on Tinder a few months ago."

I laughed. "Yeah, I swipe right on everyone I know when I see them on there. It's just polite."

We kept talking. We talked about Leonard Cohen's death album, and a particular song which seemed, at first listen, like an overly simple group of lyrics, until he got to the lines, "If the sea were sand alone / and the flowers made of stone"—throwaway bullshit, we agreed, until it came to the kicker, "And no one that you hurt could ever heal." A terrifying world.

A guy who I didn't like and didn't trust came into the bar, a sketchy gay guy who's always offering me drugs I've never heard of, which I always refuse, because I hadn't done anything but drink and smoke weed since my serious addiction days in my teens and early twenties. <<Redacted>> bought some pills off of him, and I took two without checking to see what they were. We got in <<redacted>>'s car, and I opened my mouth and told him to put another on my tongue. His fingers were in my mouth as I sucked the pill out of them. There is this thing that happens when my humanity gets challenged, like I felt it had in class earlier that day. I self-destruct. It's a long, continuous loop of trauma reactions that I honed over my entire abusive childhood, where instead of dealing with the things I had no way of escaping or processing, I did whatever it took to hurt myself with little regard to how it might also hurt others. I could feel myself doing it then, but there wasn't much I could do to stop it. I was too drunk, too upset, too frustrated and furious. <<Redacted>> and I went to his friend's house, and I remember filing down the plaster of a sculpture in the attic. The next thing I remember clearly is waking up naked, stuck to the leather couch in the living room, sore and unsure what had happened the night before.

"Did we fuck?" I said when I realized <<redacted>> was sleeping on the floor next to the couch. He was in pajamas. I'd passed out naked, maybe during or maybe after whatever had happened, and he had been awake and conscious enough to put his clothes back on.

"Just fumbled around," he said. "I was too drunk."

"Did you use a condom?"

"I don't think it got that far."

"I've got to go," I said.

I got up, feeling shame and guilt and a lot of other feelings I couldn't wait to stuff down with more whiskey. I pulled on my clothes and walked out of the house, down the street, to a bagel shop where I got coffee and a lox bagel, got on the bus, went back home. When I went into the bathroom to shower and change my clothes, I saw that I was bleeding. I noted it as an abstraction, showered, and went into my university, where I had meetings with professors and department heads about the incident that had happened in class the day before. The fallout had been a slew of emails, at that point, where one professor and the department head of the Cleveland university called out the incident for how poorly the other professor had handled it, helping navigate my friend and I to solutions that didn't involve us going back to a broken workshop environment. I was barely able to hold myself together, blamed my dragging inflection and general lack of composure on having come down with a cold because of stress. I went home, called off work, and slept all the time for several days, only waking up to answer more emails.

■

My friends are all friends with <<redacted>>. One friend referred to him as "the nicest of the creeps." He was around a lot, if not friends with everyone, then certainly tolerated by everyone. It was agreed that <<redacted>> often played the role of devil on one's shoulder, and nights my friends hung out with him often ended up at strip clubs and dive bars, doing cocaine in cars outside them. I wasn't worried about it then, often ended up in these cars myself (though I don't go to strip clubs and prefer downers), wondering what I was doing there. <<Redacted>>, though he has the same degree I do, only sometimes acquiesces to the fact that he's a writer. He's published about two short stories and his unpublished thesis is public in the university library's online system. He's a good writer and invested in famous writers in a way I'm not really, a way that I reserve for sadboy singers and rock musicians. <<Redacted>>'s invested in those same singers, though, and in film, and in the arts in general in an intelligent and obsessive way. He's also probably the only person I know in the area who's as depressed and suicidal as me.

At the point after which I woke up naked on his friend's couch,

I still didn't like him. I told my friends about the incident with a massive amount of shame. I wasn't unconvinced he was a neo-Nazi, partly because he always defaulted to Bowie's creepiest, swastika-laden songs at karaoke, partly because he was continually making jokes about the Holocaust.

Still, my friends' endorsement of him as not really a bad guy meant I spent a lot of time with him. We hung out at the same bar and would run into each other a lot. One night, I ran into <<redacted>> and a girl he was dating at the bar. She was cute, younger, probably too good for him. I flirted with them both. When he left for the bathroom, I kissed her. She stroked the side of my face saying I was such a soft boy, so gentle. When she went to the bathroom, I pushed <<redacted>> up against the wall and kissed him aggressively. They both came back to my place because they were too drunk to drive. I was drunk, too.

The three of us were on my futon, and I was making out with <<redacted>> when she said she was too drunk, too jealous, and wanted to go to sleep. <<Redacted>> and I both went to sleep, too, him on the futon and me in my bed, but I woke up and woke him up and we left to go to Taco Bell. I looked over at him in the passenger seat of my car and said, "I want to die."

He replied, "I want to die, too."

I started my car and he added, "Maybe not like this, in a car crash."

On the way back, in the parking lot outside my apartment, when he was sitting in the passenger seat of my car, he took his dick out and told me to suck it, which I did. We ended up in the back seat, amid a pile of garbage and drawings from students for whom I'd done a class visit about being a writer. <<Redacted>> fucked me with his hands, on top of me, slapping and choking me. After, we sat there for a minute, the shitty tacos congealing in a bag in the front seat, and <<redacted>> said, "We're a lot alike."

"No," I said. "I try to be a good person."

"Oh, so do I," he said. "And here we are."

■

One day <<redacted>> told one of our friends, "If Alex and I dated, we would both be dead in a month." I didn't think this was an unfair assessment. There were times it felt like we were playing chicken to see which one of us would fall completely into the void first.

I play this game a lot, with a lot of different people. I seek out the most depressed and broken people I can find, we express this mutually to one another, and the game is on. If the goal of chicken is to take it as far as you can without dying, it's easy to say I am very good at it, because I never look away from the edge. During the game, there's your usual amount of sad drinking, drugging, fucking, suicidal gestures—all the things most people do to mildly play along. Inevitably, my refusal to back off and self-preserve scares everyone. I always end up winning, and I always end up alone, because it turns out that most people do not like that void as much as they think they do. They do not really want to fall into it.

But I have always found it the safest, darkest, and most comfortable place, a closet you lock yourself in during a thunderstorm. If this sounds like cliché, it's because refusal to address trauma sticks you in a loop that is entirely predictable. A lot of people know when to veer away from it. I do not. I never have. I am trying so hard to learn.

It's also incredibly hard to judge people who you play this game with, the longer you play it, especially those who may not even have the self-awareness to understand that it's the game you're playing. After everything that happened, I care about <<redacted>>, now, though I haven't always. I hope he has the good sense to veer away, to quit playing this game entirely.

■

It was rape.

The first time I tried to write this essay, I wrote about how fucking <<redacted>>, who I knew was bad for me, was better than a lot of things that have happened in my life. It doesn't surprise me, now, that when piecing together my feelings about our friendship, I referred back to an incident that happened when I was in my early twenties.

I was in active addiction the first time I was raped. I was twenty-three years old. I was heartbroken, having just ended a nearly five-year relationship with someone I thought I'd be with for life, and in my heartbreak, I drank nearly every night and did opiates as often as I could find them. I started hanging out with this guy who I had known when I was eighteen and even more of a mess than I was at twenty-three. He was older, over thirty, and married to someone my age.

One night, when his wife was in bed and I was drinking with him, I passed out on his living room floor. I think I had taken Vicodin that night, as well. I know I drank more than I should have. I woke up to him having pulled down my pants, to him guiding his penis inside me. He fucked me for about thirty seconds before pulling out and cumming all over me. Then he apologized.

"I'm sorry. I'm so sorry."

I didn't know what he was apologizing for. I fell back asleep on the floor.

In the year that followed, I became sexually involved with both him and his wife. I spent almost every day with them. I slept in their bed. I remember that you could see over the whole small, awful town they lived in from their bedroom window. I remember the gauzy white curtains blowing around in the breeze. I remember fucking him while she was at work one day, and asking, "Does your wife care that you sleep with other people?" and him saying what he did was his own business. I remember him touching me, me saying no, and him insisting, "Your mouth is saying no, but your body's not."

One day he kicked me out of his house for being on heroin in the morning. I don't remember if I ever talked to him again.

I put that anecdote in the original version of this essay to say, this isn't that bad. This isn't that. But I realize now that I felt compelled to tell that story because it's part of my trauma pattern. Someone treats me poorly, and I fawn over them, convincing myself I love them sometimes, letting them keep on treating me poorly until they get sick of the whole thing. Until I begin to express that maybe things aren't right. Until I begin to talk, bewildered, about what has been happening.

It was rape.

I'm comfortable saying this now. It took me a year and half of getting closer and closer to the person who did it to even begin to look at that phrase clearly, to try it on, to say it to myself.

■

One drunken night, when we were fucking around in my bed, <<redacted>> said, "We should try this sometime after we drink one glass of wine." It seemed sweet and absurd, and both of us probably knew it would never, ever happen. I believe, but cannot remember exactly, that was the night that <<redacted>> really gently kissed my stomach after we fucked.

■

It was rape.

There's a detail I can't get out of my head no matter how hard I try not to think about it. That first night we had sex, I woke up naked under a blanket. <<Redacted>> had pajamas on. I had passed out sometime during the whole incident, and he had been awake and aware enough to get up and get dressed.

One day, a good day when I was sober, I texted <<redacted>> something along the lines of how suicide was an inevitability for me, how I would definitely do it with an overdose that looked accidental, and how I hoped that when it happened he'd do me a favor and tell people he thought it was an accident. That things had been better, that my writing was gaining traction and success, and that my death was just me being a drugged-out fool. I told him I wanted him to reassure people of that so they wouldn't feel bad, like they had wasted their efforts on the many times they'd tried to help.

"Alex, are you okay?" he texted back hours later.

I told him I was. That I was having a great day, in fact. But the good days just made things like this clearer.

He told me he'd woken up to my text around noon. That it was an awful thing to wake up to, but that he totally understood. I told him, yes, I knew, and that was why I had texted it to him and not someone else.

■

The last time <<redacted>> and I fucked around, I said, after cumming, with some surprise, "You know, I really like you."

"I know you do," he said. Our mutual friends had been gossiping about our friendship, alternately telling each of us the other was in love with the other and saying to people who are not us how toxic and horrible the whole thing seemed.

"We started off kinda rough," I said.

"You did," he corrected. "I thought, 'There is a person who's just like me, who's been to the same concerts as me, who listens to the same music as me, who I understand.' You thought I was a goddamn neo-Nazi."

"Well, it's different now," I said. I put my pants on. I looked out the window, where the sky had lightened.

He began talking about a friend who had killed herself. After everything falls apart, after I send <<redacted>> an early, angry version of this essay, he will say that my bringing this conversation up again is me trying to claim the pain of a situation I wasn't there for, that I didn't understand at all. But it seemed so crystal clear to me in that moment that we were both irreparably broken, dealing with all sorts of unresolved trauma; it hung in the gray-lit air. It was a few days later when I told <<redacted>> that I didn't want to get fucked up and fuck him anymore, and he stopped speaking to me, began accusing me of sexually assaulting his girlfriend at the bar that night and getting him fired from his teaching job.

"I know," I said, to his story of loss. We sat there for a while, quietly, empty White Claw cans on my table, White Claw and vodka buzzing our heads, books scattered all around, my cat glaring at him from a corner. We had been reading each other classic short stories and drinking Scotch earlier. He wanted to go home. I insisted we get more and more fucked-up as the night went on. He stuck around. He seemed to want to be there, and not. I could understand that feeling.

"It's daybreak," I said. "Let's go get breakfast."

We drove, then pulled over and walked when a cop car started driving behind us. We sat in an empty diner. I said, "I don't know why I ever married my ex-wife."

"Isn't that what we all want?" he said. He really did want that, I think. Not the general drug-taking and sad fucking he and I both do. He wanted someone to love him, that he could love in return. Maybe I want that. Maybe I won't ever let myself try it again, either. Maybe that's something that seemed to start with my failed marriage but started a long time before that.

"I was in love with her. What a stupid reason to marry someone."

"It sounds like a good reason."

"It made me not able to see who she was. She ruined my life," I said.

"I know," he said.

On the walk back, I nearly threw up and told him to shut up while I fought my roiling stomach outside his car. He said he was going to drive home, and I told him he absolutely could not, and had to sleep for a few hours on my couch until he sobered up. Which he did. When he woke up, I offered him coffee, even though he never drinks it.

"I've got to go," he said.

And he did.

∎

This is a story about sexual assault. It's also a story about a lot of sex, with the same person, which wasn't sexual assault. It's a story about the kind of friend you make when you both very much want to die. It's a story about when your life and someone else's life meet at a point where they're both so out of control it creates a perfect storm. This perfect storm ended up with most of my friends in the literary scene in Cleveland not speaking to me when I began to process how fucked-up things were between me and <<redacted>>. It ended up with a lot of things broken in ways that can't be fixed. It's a story about choice. It's also a story about when your choices are made for you by traumas you can't get ahold of easily or change. For both of us.

∎

<<Redacted>> is a deeply fucked-up person who has no idea how to break out of his cycles. He's someone who makes bad decisions, over and over, because he cannot imagine living life in a way that

doesn't revolve around them. Despite my understanding that now, he's someone whose hurt and brokenness I don't truly understand, and which I probably made worse, in my own way.

It was rape.

Both of these things can be true.

IN A PARALLEL UNIVERSE

The Multiverse Theory suggests that the universe is infinite and that, being infinite, every configuration of particles must repeat multiple times. Think of it as a deck of cards. You can only throw out so many pairs until they start repeating. And so, some believe, infinite versions of ourselves are out navigating worlds just a little to the left or right of ours.

■

In this universe, things went the way they did.

■

In another universe, I just went home that day after class. I cried and I got up and went through my life having been hurt but not deeply scarred.

■

In another universe, I wasn't taught by the people who raised me not to trust what I knew to be true inside myself. In that universe,

I became a boy at five, grew up without trauma, could feel the things inside me without question. In that universe, when I met him and my instincts told me to stay away, I listened. In that universe, I am not broken, and I trust myself. None of this ever happened.

■

In another universe, I wake up the next morning and say, "What the fuck did you do to me last night?" He denies any wrongdoing, just like he will do in this universe, a year later, when I confront him at a bar about how I was bleeding the next day and he says, "Maybe you did that to yourself." But I don't let him deny it. In this universe, I beat the fuck out of him the next morning. I am the one who goes to jail.

■

In another universe, one day when we are in bed, drunk, I say, "This is going to end with both of us hurt so badly. We're both in so much pain. We're bound to hurt one another severely." But it happens, anyway. All of it happens, anyway. These words, this self-awareness at the time, this warning we both should and don't heed, is the only thing that's different in that universe.

■

In another universe, I trust myself, I listen to my instincts, I stay away, but all of this still happens because there is a moment I let my guard down, and that is the moment when he assaults me. In that universe, I wake up bleeding and I know right away what happened. I go to the hospital, and get a rape kit, and go to the police. In that universe, he is in prison.

■

In another universe, the sex gets more violent than usual one night, and I am a statistic, another trans person lost to cis violence. In this universe, my rapist faces no consequences.

■

In another universe, I am still the broken person I was when he assaulted me, but the next time I see him, when the word "rape" is still buried in my mind, when he comes home with me, when we sit on my wooden floor and play rummy, when he lays on his back and pulls my wrists so I am laying on top of him, I laugh and say, "What are we doing here?" and then we don't do anything. In that universe, because I didn't sleep with him for eighteen months after the rape, people believe me when I say it was rape.

■

In another universe, I do not have friends who are friends with him because he is so funny and irreverent. He still assaults me, but I figure out much sooner this time that that's what it was. I am believed.

■

In another universe, I have top surgery a long time before I move to Ohio. The assault does not happen.

■

In another universe, I found a doctor who prescribed me the antidepressants I needed for twenty years before I got to Ohio, and I don't want to die when I meet him. He can't magnet to this death wish. And so, I don't keep fucking him because he makes sex and death feel close together. In this universe, when I say rape, I am believed.

▪

In another universe, when I go the police, and the police push the case through to prosecution, the prosecutor is a woman who takes the case instead of a man who says it's "not clear-cut enough" to take. In this universe, he is in prison, and I still tread water for a long time before I begin to take steps to heal. But I do heal. And I know that he will never do it again.

▪

In another universe, I don't expect things to be any different for me than they are for everyone who comes forward about rape. I am not destroyed when my community fails me. I am not hurt when a professor I admired greatly helps sweep the whole incident under the rug in my MFA community. I am not surprised when everyone's judgement turns on me. I expect it when the magazine who printed the essay about my rape posts a public retraction of it on the internet as a part of their court settlement with my rapist.

In this universe, I was still raped, but I knew better than to expect anyone's support.

▪

In another universe, I am not an addict. I say no when he offers me drugs. If he gives them to me anyway, if he assaults me anyway, then at least in that universe I am believed.

In another universe, I attempt suicide in the aftermath of all of it and succeed.

In another universe, he is a little less broken. When he sees me in the bar that night, upset, angry, hurt, he recognizes it for what it is and instead of taking advantage of my emotional state, walks me home, gives me a hug, says goodnight.

In another universe, I went to Detroit instead of Cleveland, like I planned. None of this ever happens in that universe. Something better, or maybe something worse, happens there.

In another universe, the assault happens, I sleep with him for eighteen months afterwards, but when I finally call the first incident rape, he hears me and says, "I'm sorry I hurt you." He understands that he must get better and he does. This is the universe I wanted, because I couldn't really imagine any better outcome than both of us healing.

In another universe, I drop out of grad school the first year, the way I wanted to, and I move back to New York. None of this ever happens.

■

I look and I look. I look at it from all angles. I look at all the possibilities. And yet. Here I am. It was always this way. It always will be.

THE THIRTY STEPS OF REPORTING A RAPE AS A TRANSGENDER ANARCHIST

1. Think about whether it was rape for a long time. When people tell you they are pretty sure you were raped, say, "But I took the drugs." (See: "A Brief History of Assault")

2. Wonder if the lies he tells you about yourself that you know are not true are, in fact, true.

3. Wonder if he knows how severely you have been gaslit most of your life from your abusive family. Did you tell him? You don't remember. You remember he has been abused. Maybe he can make a reasonable assumption. (See: "The Color of the Cast")

4. Be angry at everyone who knows you both.

5. Be angrier.

6. When people finally back you up, when they finally make statements and take your side, listen as a friend tells you all that your rapist worked in the university's law school as a graduate student and has lawyer friends. Watch as people take down their statements. Say you don't blame them.

7. When women come forward, several women, telling you that he assaulted them or a friend, decide you have to do something.

8. Think about it some more: you are an anarchist. You don't believe in solving problems in communities with the police. You do not want the police coming to the doors of your friends, who are mostly minorities. But, you think, this might be the only way to protect them and you, and to make sure it doesn't keep happening.

9. Take an Uber to the police station. Stand in the waiting room because of COVID-19. Say, in front of everyone else there, "I was raped, and I want to make a report."

10. Get referred to a detective at the justice center downtown.

11. Get a little pamphlet that tells you what to expect. Read it. Throw it away. Retain nothing.

12. Have nightmares. Wake up into panic attacks. (See: "Waking Up in the Night")

13. Ride your Vespa down to the justice center. Wander around the floors, asking the way. Get lost. Get lost again. Finally find the detective's office. Speak to the victim advocate. Take the Capri Sun she offers you. "It helps," she says. Then: "Just tell him the truth. Tell him what happened. And you don't have to worry about the rest."

14. Worry about the rest as she shows you the steps of what will come next.

15. Speak to the detective. Tell him you were bleeding and when he asks from where, use the word "rectum," although you don't remember ever using that word before in your life. Tell him you kept sleeping with him. Tell him about how your C-PTSD makes you hide the truth from yourself, sometimes. Tell him that is how you survived for so long. (See: "It Was Rape")

16. Cry back in the hallway.

17. Go home and have nightmares that your rapist blows his brains out. You do not want this. Wake up from them and write poems. (See: "The Night My Rapist Dies in a Dream")

18. Wake up to panic attacks. (See: "Waking Up in the Night")

19. Get Valium from a friend for when you wake up from panic attacks but take all twenty-five of them at once when you are drinking whiskey because, really, you still want to die.

20. Sign away your protections from talking to a therapist you spoke to after the rape.

21. Wait to hear back from the detective.

22. Wait more.

23. Call your rapist's mother and tell her that her son is a rapist one day when you are in a shitty hotel in Youngstown, Ohio. Hear her gasp. Keep talking, not realizing she has hung up on you. (See: "Waking Up in the Night")

24. Hear from a new victim advocate. The police have been doing training and the case is still being investigated.

25. Hear from the victim advocate again. The detective has adamantly pushed the case through to prosecution. She says, "We love to hear news like this."

26. Get a call from a 216 number one day at work. Step outside. Hear the detective tell you that he spoke to everyone you told him was involved. That the rapist's best friend verified your story. Then hear him say that, despite this, prosecution has declined to take the case and the criminal investigation is over.

27. Have nightmares. Wake up into panic attacks.

28. Repeat.

29. Repeat.

30. Repeat.

THE NIGHT MY RAPIST DIES IN A DREAM

In my dream, the detective is an old man from the bar I drink at in the early afternoon. The detective says, "It was only a matter of time before he blew his head off." I drive by the house, and I see the shattered window, stained red around the jagged, the burst of brains on the sidewalk below. There is a boy, inside, his brother, his face a gift of shock.

I think in my dream, *it is over. I did this. I will never listen to that album we both loved again even though I loved it first.*

The brother begins to clean the blood up.

I think in my dream, *he's dead our mouths were pressed together I have held his body momentarily* when the detective asks I don't know what color his eyes are when the detective asks I say his beard is stupid I never traced his spine we mostly slept drunkenly in our clothes.

The blood is the color of the tulip that exploded from the ground this spring and fell under the late-season snows and sprang back up again without argument from anyone.

I move through a senseless night. In the distortionless day the victim advocate sat silently beside me. In the day I cried in the hallway before the detective appeared. In the day I said *I don't trust the system* and the advocate touched her brown skin and said she didn't either. In the day I said *I fucked him for a year afterwards* and watched the detective's eyes dart away from me. In the day there are ten steps to reporting this kind of crime and I am so afraid.

Next to the blood on the sidewalk it is dawn. The brother has cleaned the room. He sits on the floor of the glistening world.

WHEN THE DETECTIVE COMES TO MY FRONT PORCH

My doormat says *Come Back With A Warrant.* I hide it before the detective comes. I sign away all my protected privacies from speaking to my therapist. The detective asks where I work and when I answer he mentions a beer and donut pairing place across the street. I talk with the advocate for ten minutes about my favorite donuts in town while the detective says nothing, maybe wondering, like I am, what he's gotten himself into. The doormat says, *You are a hypocrite you are a failure you are talking to the police the police are on your porch you are talking to them like friends.* I mention that one of the women who my rapist has abused has agreed to be part of the investigation. The advocate is a different person this time, a white woman who looks like a cop, too. The doormat raises a cry. *You call yourself an anarchist you tried so many ways you stuck to nothing you are a hypocrite you are a failure.* I wanted him to apologize I wanted him to get therapy I wanted him to see the wake of destruction in his drive to end his own life I wanted this to be okay I would have taken the apology and arm wrestled the rest of the aggression out really I would have I would have had a fistfight outside one of the readings we both go to I would have wrestled the remaining anger into the muddy spring night a storm cloud settling into the atmosphere it could have been better for both of us. The detective looks relieved as I change the subject from donuts. He has been trained to make small talk, to make people comfortable. I am not comfortable. There are wraps and gloves and a heavy bag on my porch and maybe he wonders why someone would rape someone who could throw a punch. The doormat says, *All those times you said Fuck The Police, screaming in the streets and holding cells.* They leave and I walk inside. The doormat has fallen silent. We have both said enough.

RESPONSIBLE

Found Piece from Sarah Polley's memoir *Run Towards the Danger*:

*Exploding bombs, space, moonwalking. It would all be per-
fectly safe, I was told. I couldn't breathe. There was chaos. How
lightly my safety and sense of security had been taken. It's hard
to calculate whether they were worth the price of hell. The
out-of-control mad white male. It was hard for me to see how
responsible ▬▬▬▬▬▬ was. I am struck by how many
times I told him I don't hold him responsible. It was hopeless for
me to imagine him taking responsibility.*

■

In the months following my public coming out about the assault,
I read a lot about abusive men.

There is the story of the young women who went public about
their English teacher who groomed them, one after another. They
came forth when he wrote a book and the coverage of it was relentless. Though the person who assaulted me will likely never write
anything much, and he will never be covered in the *New York
Times*, and he will never be plastered on news and television—he is

a thirty-something adjunct who lives with his mother—there was a different kind of relentlessness that was happening to me. In the small Ohio city I lived in, near where he had been born and lived his whole life, there were reminders of him everywhere. There were his friends he'd gone to strip clubs with making comments about literary scandals on Twitter, about how to believe survivors, and how it was always women and nonbinary people who came forward to fight rapists—all while spreading rumors about me to everyone we both knew. There was the local press, whose head had run a reading series with my rapist, who had been a big part of the reason my rapist was in my life, publishing a book by a rape survivor as if the publisher hadn't *also* been ruining my life with rumors. There were women coming forward to me by DM, by anonymous message, by sitting down with me over drinks and telling me what he had done to them. When I began yelling on the internet one day after my grad program promoted the new play of the man whose couch I'd been raped on, I got a message from a number I didn't know. It was the man whose couch I'd been raped on. He said he believed me. He said he wasn't friends with <<redacted>> anymore. He said that <<redacted>> had aestheticized catastrophe and there was no changing him. One day, a year later, when I was sitting on the patio of a bar, I see the man whose couch I was raped on with his friends. He does not see me. They begin talking about <<redacted>>, about someone who'd sucked his dick when he exposed himself to them, as he did frequently. They were doubled over in laughter. The rape reverberated into every corner of my life. It was inescapable. I didn't think I'd ever get away from it unless I left town entirely, which I eventually did.

■

There is *Lolita*. When I reread this book, I see how abuse works—not just the violence of it but the dependence of it. In the months after my rapist assaulted me, we had sex over and over. There was a lot of sexual pleasure on my part. I would think about these encounters for days after. But far away from my rapist, having come out with the accusation months before, I began to wonder if the moments I had felt empathy for him or moments I had enjoyed being around him hadn't been designed to foster this sort of dependence. This sort of bond between abuser and abused. I thought about the music we both loved, I thought about the stories he shared of his own pain. And while I didn't doubt they were *true*, it was also clear that any attachment I felt to him through these things was that way by design.

My friend Vivien pointed all of this out to me, too. She said that probably none of it was conscious, just as my need for self-destruction that had drawn me closer to my rapist wasn't something I sat down and calculated. "He got sexual pleasure out of it," she said, when I asked what someone could get from manipulating me.

"Hardly," I said. "He could never get hard, so I don't know how much sexual pleasure there is in getting your limp dick sucked."

"He got an image of himself, then," she went on. "In his head he's some guy who fucks a lot, but he has a limp dick in reality. But fucking around with you, having everyone know about it, made the image he has of himself seem more real. He's some emotionally stunted, spoiled jerk with mommy and daddy issues, but fucking you he got to slum it in your depression and pretend he's an artist with deep emotional torture."

The thing she said that sticks with me the most, though, is that neither of us really calculated our interaction—we both simply got something out of it what we wanted, that we were driven to. She was careful to state that she didn't believe any of it was my fault. But I think there's something there. I think that is how abuse works some of the time. There is something that keeps you in it long after you rationally know better.

■

The last thing I read that stayed with me was an excerpt from Sarah Polley's memoir in which she talks about the abuse she faced at the hands of Terry Gilliam, the film director, when she was a child filming *The Adventures of Baron Munchausen*. She talks about how much trauma and terror she was subjected to, and how it was all sanctioned by everyone around her in service of what was considered Gilliam's "mad genius." She was a small piece of collateral damage when the big picture was artistic greatness. I didn't relate much to that part of it, but I froze when I read about the emails she had sent to him. Over and over, in them, she absolves him of any responsibility.

"Because he was so childlike and full of genuine wonder, it was hard for me, for many years, to see how responsible Terry Gilliam was for the terror of being on that set. And so, I blamed my parents. I'm struck by how many times in my emails to him I make sure to tell him I don't hold him responsible and lay the blame at my parents' feet."

I thought back to the text messages I had sent my rapist, the ones he would later use to bring me to court for defamation. In the days after he raped me, while I was in and out of sleep from the drugs he had given me, I wrote to him asking if we'd used a condom the night he'd raped me. "I want to stress, it was all consensual from what I remember," I said. I went on to make sure he was okay, as he might have been as high as me. He assured me he was. I don't even know, now, if he took any of the drugs he gave me that night.

But what I do know is that I felt as if I had to reassure him. I hadn't said no, right? I'd taken the drugs, right? I put the blame squarely on my own shoulders. He had just been there, at the moment, and if I didn't say no, well, that was my own fault, not his.

■

Two years after I came forward about the rape, a year and a half after I published the essay "It Was Rape," a friend messaged me on Facebook. She is a friend from high school, she doesn't know the man who raped me, so I knew I wouldn't be blindsided by being drawn back into the situation again. But she told me something that made me realize how common the things that happened to me are.

"Years ago," she said, "I was really drunk and a friend's friend offered to take me home. Everyone assured me he was a good guy, he wouldn't try anything, I'd be safe. I woke up naked the next day and had no idea how I got there. You know the four Fs of PTSD? Well, I fawned hard. I dated him for two years after. It wasn't until I read your essay that I realized that didn't matter in the scope of things—he'd still raped me. Your essay made me realize that. And I'm sure I'm not the only one that happened for."

■

In the year that my rapist brings charges against me in court, the whole country gleefully watches the Johnny Depp/Amber Heard defamation trial while memes proliferate on the internet. She is a liar. She is mentally ill. She defecated in his bed. All these things are meant to discredit her, to make her less than human. I am familiar with this tactic.

The general concept of how an abuser brings false claims against the abused is called DARVO: deny, attack, and reverse victim and offender. A website that lays out the process of DARVO tells me that common accusations from the offender look like:

- "You're a psycho."
- "You're an alcoholic or a drug addict."
- "You've made these claims before."
- "You asked for this/wanted me to do it."
- "You never said 'no.'"

I see every one of these claims in my rapist's court case against me. He uses the essay I published on my mental health because of my childhood gaslighting from family against me. He uses posts I made in the wake of my assault by my ex-wife. He tells me how complicit I am in his abuse of me and tells others that I am the one who sexually abused him.

While I read these things, I watch the entirety of the internet, even many people I love, become subsumed in the media storm that accuses Amber Heard of exactly these things. My rapist is not a famous person, and he does not have the power to plant such lies in the media like Johnny Depp does. Still, I watch people I love rail against and take joy in the dehumanization of Amber Heard, and it terrifies me every day.

■

My lawyer, Tyler, reassures me that it doesn't matter what I said the next day. He reassures me of this even through women who have been through what I've been through have already mapped this ground. He reassures me that even if I had said I was going out to have sex with my rapist the day before (which I hadn't), having sex with someone when they can't stand is still, legally, rape. He talks to me about how people know things they didn't know before #MeToo now, about how they understand it sometimes takes time to understand you've been raped. He reassures me at every turn, but I still live in fear. I live in fear of facing cis men in the jury. I live in fear of how transphobic the jury will be, there in Ohio. I am sure there will be no trans people on it. I imagine the things I will say on the witness stand. I imagine the things that <<redacted>> will say.

One thing I cannot ever imagine is him taking responsibility for what he has done.

RUNNING CHECKLISTS

Is He As Bad As You Think He Is?

YES

- That time you called him a cis man and he said, "Am I?", because he knew you believed that gender identification comes from self, and you wouldn't argue his actual gender if he said he wasn't cis just to make a point.
- That time he went on a date and told you and your friends he couldn't get hard and used the term "skull-fucked" to describe what he did with the woman he went out with.
- The time your friend who you love and trust told you that he said, of a trans woman, "You know, she has a dick," for no reason other than to be, himself, a dick.
- He hits you so fucking hard. It's not what you want. You have to correct him every time.
- The weird thing he does where he makes fun of his mother (who he lives with) all the time, mimicking her voice and mannerisms—it's creepy and misogynistic.
- All your friends—your real friends, who you love, who love you—hate him.
- Even your good-times friends, while they are friends with him, agree he is a fucking creep. One of them says he "puts on his human act" around you, and that's why you like him.

NO

- He is as broken as you.
- You feel empathy for this brokenness.
- When you are alone together, he doesn't seem as bad, not all the time, anyway.

Should You Keep Having Sex with Him?

YES

- You believe in casual sex with friends, so it's not like it has to mean anything, be good, or go anywhere.
- He makes you cum with his hands.
- You feel bad every time you have sex with him but it's not like you don't already feel bad, anyway.
- In your very fucked up way, you come to care for him.

NO

- Almost every time you do, you wake up bleeding.
- That first time—
- You don't like him much, not for a long time, anyway.
- You feel bad every time you have sex with him.
- You have other sexual relationships that you get a lot more out of.
- He never uses condoms, ever.
- He has casual sex with lots of people, not using condoms.
- Every time you do, you tell your friends with so much shame and embarrassment.

Should You Keep Living?

YES

- The people who love you, who you love back, in the limited fashion you can
- Your niece and nephew
- You like riding your Vespa.
- You feel like you have so much more to write.
- Your cat needs you. When she dies, your dog needs you even more.

NO

- The depression hasn't gone away in twenty years.
- The depression will never go away.
- You are a black hole of need, and nothing can fill it up.
- You feel like shit about yourself all the time.
- Everything you do makes you feel worse.
- You always make the decision towards chaos.
- You're just a fucking junkie.
- Maybe people will read your work if you're gone?
- Your family hates you.
- So many people who said they loved you were not in it for the long haul.
- There's no one much who will miss you.
- You hate school.
- There is no place for you.
- You've failed at everything.
- You will keep failing.
- You have ruined everything.
- None of it matters.
- None of it matters.
- You can barely breathe with all the energy your depression takes up.
- You cannot imagine life any other way.
- You missed your appointment.
- You lost a friend.
- You got high *again.*
- You're always drunk.
- You said something stupid.
- The list goes on.

PART THREE

THE MAGICIAN.

"Most modern images of the trump follow Waite's wizard, raising a magic wand to bring into reality the spirit force – the energy of life in its most creative form. He holds the wand carefully, aware of the psychic power the Fool carried so lightly on his shoulder. Thus, the Magician, as the beginning of the Major Arcana proper, represents consciousness, action, and creation. He symbolizes the idea of manifestation, this is, making something real out of the possibilities of life. Therefore, we see the four emblems of the Minor Arcana lying on a table in front of him. He not only uses the physical world for his magical operations (the four emblems are the objects used by all wizards in their rituals), but he also creates the world, in the sense of giving life meaning and direction."

—RACHEL POLLACK, *Seventy-Eight Degrees of Wisdom:*
A Tarot Journey to Self-Awareness

WHEN I DECIDE BECOMING A WITCH WILL SAVE ME

My rapist once admitted that he does black magic on his exes, asking me not to tell anyone. I am telling you now. He said it was easy he looked up the process on the internet went to a field he said it worked but he didn't have the energy to do it anymore. I told him this was why his life is a hurricane of chaos why he can't get his dick hard. These things always come back to you.

During the two weeks I don't get out of bed to shower I start reading my cards every day. I pull Judgment over and over. Judgment is final Judgment a symphony of trumpets an appearance of angels the world our dance creates falling away. Sometimes it has been the far future but now always the center of the spread. I am in a universe winding down I am grasping at the falling tendrils I am afraid to look to the sky.

A dear friend says the monogrammed handkerchief he left behind was a red flag I say it is the thing I wrap in anger while cursing his name binding him to himself putting it in a box I might bury or throw in a lake.

Sometimes I dream of him healed, of me unwrapping it, giving it back.

A BRIEF HISTORY OF MAGIC

This morning, sitting down to write, I decided to consult my cards first. The cards I read were the Starman deck, a deck created by Davide De Angelis, an artist who worked closely with David Bowie. I began using this deck before I blessed it and, I believe as a result of this aberration in custom, the deck now insists I cleanse it thoroughly before each time I use it for divination for others. When I read from it without doing so, the results are scattered, hard to read. But when I light a stick of Palo Santo given to me by a witch of Mexican heritage, taking a few cards out and holding them over the smoke, then a few more, then a few more until the entire deck has been touched by the sacred smoke of the palo santo stick, the readings become clear and unambiguous. This is how magic works, sometimes. The magic teaches you through trial and error. There are spells and traditions that have been passed down through the ages, tested for you, that arrive like a rental car ready to move you to your destination with little worry or trouble. But the kind of magic I practice most, and love thoroughly, is arrived at through mistakes. In this way, it is more like learning to bake was for me. Sometimes, I would head forward with a plan, spend great amounts of time and money and effort on it, only to have it fail, the results inedible. As I learned, I began to understand intuitively where I had made errors, correct them before trying again. I understood which parts of the recipe had wiggle room to improvise in. The end results were recipes of my own, which had maybe started in a book or on a website, but which I had altered, added my own flair and style and tastes to. These are the best kinds of recipes. Similarly, magic with your own spin is the best kind, the kind you write down in a notebook and pass down to someone, someday.

I won't go too much into what the cards said, other than that they energized me, and also reminded me of the great use sadness can be put to in connecting others and bringing about understanding.

■

I bought my first magic book at Walden Books in the Wyoming Valley Mall in Wilkes-Barre, Pennsylvania. It was a book of spells, and I had none of the right materials to do any of them—strange herbs, brightly colored candles—nor access, as an unemployed thirteen-year-old girl without the internet, to acquire them. I was awkward and crooked-toothed and didn't know how to brush my curly hair yet. I wanted people to see past that and love me. I wasn't above using spell work to make them do so. But I never cast any spells, anyway, and later I would learn that these were not ancient folkloric traditions but new age, crystal-collecting bullshit.

I bought my first set of tarot cards shortly thereafter, a Rider-Waite deck that I probably also got at Walden Books. I would dutifully lay out the Celtic Cross spread that was suggested in the accompanying book for friends and myself, not knowing what any of it meant, a little terrified (good Catholic that I was) of The Devil and Death cards. After a year or so, I was overwhelmed by the number of cards, sure I would never learn them in any meaningful way, and put them away.

It wouldn't be until I was nearly forty years old that I picked them up again.

■

Magic is not sleights of hand that make someone smile. This does not mean there is no laughter in magic. The night a witch friend initiated me there were rose petals and there was adorning with gold dust and summoning of energy and spilling of spoiled wine but there was also a three-person rendition of "Put It in Your Mouth," and hysterics when an unwitting delivery man from 7-Eleven walked into the end of our ceremony.

■

All over the internet, there are white people claiming to be Heyoka (sacred clown). All over the internet, there are white people claiming to be shaman. All over the internet, there are white people claiming to practice Santería. All over the internet, there are white people claiming all sorts of traditions that don't belong to them. While these designations were certainly attractive to me, I have never wanted to be a person who claimed things that weren't mine to claim. For most of my life, I thought that Catholicism, which I had been raised in, was my only option, and it was an option that had forced me out because of who I was. When I discovered that my ancestors had their own tradition, and a syncretized one no less, it was a very important moment for me. I had something I could practice without appropriation. I had something that could link me to the people I had come from, a process that had made my life fuller, and more stable. There were things I could believe in, that had been believed in for generations before Christianity, and even after it, through a combination of folk tradition and the church.

■

I had gone off my meds a few months before the most recent time I sought out mental healthcare, just before my fortieth birthday, because I was too broke to get them. After years of doctors changing my meds, I had stopped taking the mood stabilizers that didn't help a few years before, and was then only on blood pressure meds and an antipsychotic. I read an article one day about long-term use of antipsychotics causing brain damage, and between a particularly bad bout of poverty and that article, I decided to stop taking my Abilify. Within a few months, nothing made sense and I couldn't focus. I sat on the front porch of my apartment, called my best friend, and wondered aloud if I was the real problem in my life—it was after the fallout of my being sexually assaulted, when my whole life in Ohio had fallen apart. She assured me I was not.

"These people all hate me," I said, vaguely.

"Those people are assholes," she assured me. "You're not the problem. You are just in a bad place right now."

I sat there, my vision tunneling into the irrefutable notion that suicide was the only way out. I checked myself into a mental health crisis center, not quite a psychiatric hospital.

While I was in the crisis center, lying on plastic beds with plastic pillows, I looked on my Kindle for a book about Southern Italian folk tradition, and found *Italian Folk Magic* by Mary Grace Fahrun. It is a book that is based on a blog that gathered the collective wisdom from generations of Italian witches and their families. While I went to drawing groups and movie watching groups, I read about the tradition of *Stregheria*, or *Benedicaria*: the former a word we don't say, and the latter the modern, softer, less forbidden term.

I had begun practicing magic not long before this, but something finally clicked when I read this book.

■

This morning I consult my cards. I use the Modern Witch Tarot, which was given to me by my old neighbor Dani. These cards read easily for me, and when I read them, I often see the figures in the world around me: a boy in a long, black hooded down coat that resembles Death's cloak; a woman who looks for all the world like the motorcycle-straddling woman in The Chariot, and who talks to me outside a gas station about cars and motorcycles and how to fix them. I keep the cards wrapped in a French silk scarf with red poppies on it.

Today the cards tell me that running is my obstacle. I think about this a lot, how I left New York when I split up with my wife, how I ran from Geneva, Ohio, after I lost my job to workplace discrimination, how I left Cleveland, Ohio, after I was raped and wrote about the rape. Everywhere I go seems fraught. There is hope for me here, in Philadelphia. Healing as I am, going to therapy as I am, I hope to build a better life here. My new therapist and I talk all the time about how I can start over, build my community intentionally, a person at a time, rather than falling into one full of pitfalls like I did in Cleveland.

The Fool—the beginning of the journey—is in my near past and an inverted Justice is in my near future. Justice has come up a lot for my near-future card since the lawsuit started. That it's inverted brings me pause—will I settle this case, not fully receiving justice? An inverted card, to the way I read, means something is blocking the nature of this card in your life. I look for clues in the other cards.

Something is blocking balance in my subconscious, an inverted Temperance tells me, and I see in the card that holds my perception of myself that I think I am honoring tradition and ancestry (Ten of Pentacles). What if all this—the running, the spirituality, the healing—is just in my imagination? Does it matter? Did it ever?

My outcome card shows a blockage of the things I have planted, hoping for abundance. I look to my advice card and see that something is blocking my ship coming in, my luck. This is not surprising. What can I do to change my luck? I have been working at it so hard.

■

I pulled my natal chart today. I have done this several times, but I don't know the exact moment of my birth. Because I don't speak to my living family and it is not on my birth certificate, I likely won't ever know it. As near as I can tell, I am a Virgo Sun, a Taurus Moon, and a Leo Rising. There is a lot of Libra in my various houses.

I don't know what this means, other than broad strokes. Some websites recommend, when you don't know the time of your birth, that you work backwards through your life, a process called rectification, or backwards forecasting. Even Co–Star makes my head spin, so I don't think this is something I will do successfully. The stars and planets may forecast the future, but it's without the benefit of my knowledge that they do so.

A lot of people find comfort in astrology, but I don't. There may be an order to the cosmos, but it is not one that I can find for myself. Instead, I hang wooden spoons on my wall, make sure the air of the refrigerator is blowing, cleanse with the water from my kitchen sink, and cook with the fire on my stove. I sprinkle sea salt. I say prayers.

■

Before I took a genetic test that told me exactly where my family was from, I knew that we had been, in part, from Calabria, a state at the tip of the boot of Italy, bordered on the east by the Ionian

Sea. For years, whenever someone Italian would ask me where my family was from, I would say that region, and they would reply, "Ah, *testa dura*," or "Head like rock and wood." With my incredible stubbornness, I always felt very seen by this regional stereotype. It was only when I took a genetic test that I learned that my people were not just the hard-headed people of Calabria, but also Sicilians, a region with a lot of practitioners of Stregheria.

One day, when I am reading about folk tradition, I learn that Italian witches don't read tarot, they read regional playing cards from their provinces. I immediately order a deck of Sicilian playing cards. They are beautiful, small enough to hold comfortably in one hand, divided into four suits: cups, coins, swords, and clubs. One day when I am not doing so well in the mental health department, I spend all day with them, shuffling them, reading them from a book that gives me their meanings, trying to put my magic into them. I wrap them in a blue pocket square. In magic, blue is symbolic of healing. I am trying so hard to heal the broken ancestral bonds that I have no real link to.

I wish to walk along the Ionian Sea one day, to view the sea my ancestors looked at through eyes that are partially mine and partially theirs, to unlock some genetic understanding through place and water and sky. Until then, I will settle for my playing cards, imagining my ancestors shuffling, reading, foretelling. I will take magic where I can find it.

A BRIEF HISTORY OF CURSES

In Italian folk tradition, *il malocchio* is another word for "the evil eye." *Malocchio* can be put on someone through an insincere compliment (one should never thank a rival who compliments them—to not do so blocks *malocchio*), or even just a look born in envy or disgust. *Malocchio* can be detected through pouring olive oil in water and watching how it settles. *Malocchio* can be blocked several ways: wearing a cornicello, spreading salt at your front door to confuse the spirits, the person who gave it touching the forehead of the person who they gave it to, making hand gestures, touching your crotch if you're a man.

When Italian children are born, they are often given a cornicello, a necklace with a twisted horn that resembles a chili pepper, to block out the possibility of being cursed. Most of the people I know from Italian American families recognize this tradition, but my Italian grandparents were long dead by the time I was born, so I was offered no such protection. My father was someone I loved, but someone who was also abusive—and Italians believe that you can curse others with the gestures of your hands. I note this to say that, though I can't speak to truth here, I imagine one of the reasons my father never hit me while he did my siblings was that I was his child who was born without the protection of his parents.

I am not without protection, though. The writer Liz Prato, when we discussed looking for the roots of our Italian magic on Twitter, once sent me silver necklace with a cornicello on it. I wear it every day. I'm not sure if she knows what this gesture means to me, but I do know from reading her work that as someone who is adopted, she, too, might have lacked the protections of ancestors. Sometimes, we make our own magic.

■

(Use this blank space to imagine protections your ancestors would give you if they could.)

Reading about the evil eye, I am thinking not of whether I have *malocchio*, but how many times I've probably given it. That time I hated someone in my master's program. That time I broke up with my ex, Adam, at a bus stop and he freaked out about the look I was giving him. That time someone pissed me off in a kitchen I was working in. Looking at someone with disgust when they anger me is something I do a lot of. How many people have I unintentionally cursed? I think about how I truly need to fix my face. I think about how I wish I could kiss their foreheads and take the curse away. I think about how unthoughtfully I gesture with my hands, a bit frantically. I promise myself that I'll be intentional with my gestures.

■

I take a bowl and fill it with water. I take a bottle of olive oil and am careful to drop an odd number of drops in it. The drops begin to spin, coming together, reconnecting along straight paths: the evil eye is present, and this particular configuration of oil means a group of people are the culprits, spreading rumors, gossiping. I think about the recent past, and I know this is true.

I take a pair of scissors and cut the surface of the water, breaking the oil into tiny spinning beads. Will this be enough? I hope so.

■

I speak to spirits through my tarot cards. I know I am speaking to my father's mother, because that is who I call upon when I take out my cards. My ancestors speak through the images. Still, one day, when I was in a pagan shop at a tarot card club night, and the person leading the event said that we had to know who we were speaking to through our tarot cards because they were like a Ouija board, and if we spoke to someone we didn't know, the messages could be scrambled or worse, a thrill of electric shock ran through me.

I drew a card to see who I was speaking to. The Queen of Cups. My terror abated. It was just my father's mother speaking to me, after all.

■

The twenty years I dealt with chronic depression seemed like a curse to me. Would I ever be happy? Would I ever shake my suicidal ideation? It seemed like I would not.

After being misdiagnosed with bipolar disorder in my twenties and being put on antipsychotics and mood stabilizers, I was finally, at near age forty, rediagnosed with complex PTSD and chronic depression. I was put on an antidepressant. It worked.

I'll take my magic where I can get it, even if it's dispensed to me thirty pills at a time by a pharmacist at Walgreens.

■

I'm not sure if I've ever been cursed, though a lot of signs do point to it. I look these signs up on the internet and see that some of them include runs of bad luck (check), repetitive nightmares (check), recurrent headaches (check), and unshakable depression (check). It makes me wonder if the idea of curses wasn't a pre-psychological way of naming and dealing with trauma.

■

My mother often likes to repeat that when she was in the hospital, just out of labor with my oldest sibling, my sister Gina, my paternal grandmother came in the room, held Gina, and said to my still out-of-it mother, who had gone through childbirth with no sedatives or pain killers, "You had a girl for you, now have a boy for my son."

I view that as some incredibly hardcore old Italian woman shit. "She was the kind of woman who would put the evil eye on you," my mother has often said of my paternal grandmother. When my mother says "you" here, I think she means herself, more than anyone: a blond Polish woman that my father brought home, disrupting years of tradition. My mom, a strict Catholic, would probably have been mortified if my grandmother gave my siblings cornicellos. I don't speak to my siblings, so I don't know if they have them or not. I know I do not.

I don't think my grandmother cursed me, though I imagine her death might have left me without the protections I needed. I think she would have adored me, had we ever met: a curly black-haired child with the same gap from missing eye teeth as her, born with an umbilical cord around my neck, which denotes magical inclinations in Italian tradition. Someone to pass her knowledge along to. But we never met, not in real life. I call on her a lot when I do magic, and I know she is listening to me.

■

While looking up the signs of curses, I find something called a witch bottle that is meant to thwart them. I decide to make one to protect this house I've come to rest in, here in Philadelphia. It requires a bottle, some old metal nails, hair, and piss. While I squat over my toilet with the glass bottle firmly pressed against my vulva, I think how I kind of enjoy how gross it is. I use the hair I kept from when I was growing out my bleach job and had a mullet and cut it off just before a job interview. I like to think the inch of blonde represents the last of the difficult times I was in when in Ohio.

I burn a black candle on it, its wax dripping down and sealing it. I think about the person I'm moving in with me from Alabama: a young trans masculine person that I met online through fandom of one of our mutual favorite rock stars. I've always wanted to provide safe space for trans people younger than me. I'm really worried I won't do it well, but I've rented a house here with enough room for both of us, and I'm holding it until they are ready to come. They are fully grown, but I know how, at their age and queer, I needed support that no one in my life was able to give me. I don't want to be their only support, but I want to give them a soft place to land, to get out of the middle of nowhere, to be able to meet queer people and community. I want us protected, too, which is why I make the witch bottle.

I text my new roommate to tell them if they find a bottle with nails, hair, and piss in it in our house, don't touch it—it's for our protection. They text back, "Heard." I take the bottle outside where the wind gutters the candle and the steam from my piss fogs the glass. I hide it, though I won't ever say where.

HOW TO FORGET

At first, you google his name on a semidaily basis. Sometimes, because you are worried about his mental health, you add "obituary" to your search, just to be sure he hasn't killed himself. He hasn't. You wonder if the suicidality he displayed to you when you spent time together was an act, a way of trying to match your own sadness and lack of will to live. You know how often this whole thing has almost sent you over the edge, but you see no evidence of that in him.

You learn nothing when you google him. He has locked all his accounts and, from what you can tell, scraped a bunch of them. He does not publish anything new—he hasn't published since he was in graduate school a few years before you were in the same graduate school. You can't see anything about him, and you are somehow still shocked when you learn he has access to everything you say or do online despite the fact that you've long since blocked him everywhere you can. You learn this when his lawyer dumps 300+ pages of everything you've done or said or published in the last three years on your lawyer.

Slowly, you stop trying to learn things about him online.

You don't remember that night, but what you remember the most about the next day is the blood leaking out of your body.

You do something other than forget it. You make it less terrifying. You make it an expected part of such an encounter. You text him over and over in the next few days after seeing the blood, you also learn in the files his lawyer drops on your lawyer, reassuring him everything was consensual. How often have you had to reassure someone you've had consensual sex with that it was? Never, because consent is clear. What happened to you still isn't clear, partly because of the drugs, and partly because you have engaged your "fawn" defense to this new trauma. You tell him he's trouble and you like that. All of the things you see you said back then (you were still too high for days to remember saying any of it, and your phone with these text messages on it was stolen long ago) have the goal of lessening the threat. Making the enemy placated. You were bleeding. While you were saying all these things, you were still bleeding. But the thing you always loved about benzos, the reason you relapse on them that night and take them for two years after, often until you black out, is that the pain and sadness of being human disappear. You love when the world disappears, leaving you to sort it out another day. But these places of blankness are never simple or uncomplicated. You end up unraveling the things you have forgotten for years afterwards. You are still trying to unravel that night.

How can you write about what you don't remember? You write around it.

Slowly, you learn to deal with life without the blankness you desire.

You find yourself, for years afterwards, through the whole year of the court proceedings he's brought against you for defamation, talking about what is happening in your life. You have a few drinks and you tell a stranger who mentions they are in law school about your legal troubles. You go on a date and spill out the whole story while lying in your bed cuddling. You think, somehow, you have to explain it to everyone you meet. You think no one can understand you without knowing what you've been through. No matter how many times you say it, it doesn't go away.

Slowly, you learn that speaking about trauma does not always take its power away. Sometimes, it lets it hold onto your life more firmly.

Consider him. Consider him in ways he never does you: as a whole human. Consider all the things that have brought him to where he is.

There was a time, about a year after he raped you, that you felt a lot of sympathy for him. He told you about his first memory being his mother telling him she would kill him. He told you about being assaulted himself in boarding school. He told you all the time that he was as sad as you, wanted to die as much as you did. You wonder about these things now. You wonder if they were designed to make you feel empathy. You wonder if they were true. You wonder if it was a pissing contest of depression. You wonder all these things as you realize he never had any sympathy or empathy for you. When you are deep in the year of the court proceedings, he refuses to settle with you because he wants you to suffer more than you already have. You know this because his lawyer constantly tells your lawyer you haven't put "enough skin in the game," as if the whole thing is a game, as if your suffering needs to be raised like a high jump bar until you can't clear it at all.

A friend who used to be friends with him, too, says that he uses his pain to hurt others. That many of us have been through the things he has, but we don't assault other people because of it. He has lashed out with his pain against the world, against women, against you. And he feels justified in his behavior because of what he's been through. You don't, you cannot, understand this.

Slowly, you begin to see him less as a victim and more and more as a monster.

Two years after he assaults you, after your life has become a long and elaborate relapse on all the things you tried so hard to get away from for years, you relent and go to rehab. Sit in a room and work on dialectic behavioral therapy skills. Talk about what has brought you there. Start finding ways to walk with your spine straight and your shoulders not sunk in around your chest. Find ways to talk to your inner self. Find ways to let the light grow around you and inside you. Find ways to talk to your shadow self. Find ways to understand that the things that have happened to you were not your fault. Find ways to have sympathy for yourself you've never had before. Begin to feel your emotions—those terrifying tsunami things that rise up in you—without dulling them away with drugs and whiskey. Fail to understand *how* it works but feel it working on you anyway. Draw pictures in your notebook of times when you knew who you were. Write lists of the parts of yourself you want to nurture. Understand that accepting yourself and your growth are foundations for living the life you want—imagine the life you want, too, and how you will get it and keep it.

Slowly, you begin to heal. As you heal, pieces of the past fall away. You don't forget them, maybe you will never forget them, maybe there is no such thing as "how to forget." But the things that hurt you no longer fill the whole horizon.

(Use this blank space to try to forget something.)

THE DECISION

In the last months I live in Cleveland, I work at an Elks Lodge. I don't drink anymore, not really at all, not even the "once in a while, under the right conditions, and only one or two then" that I fall into when I move to Philadelphia. I enjoy my customers, especially the really, really old ones (although almost everyone is over fifty): the man with fantastic hats who drinks Michelob Ultra and requests a napkin to wipe the lip or the bottle before he drinks from it; the two women who have been best friends since childhood, who are now in their eighties, who give each other pointed jabs in the best nature possible. (One day, when the whole place is watching the Kentucky Derby, I see one of the women slap a friend of hers on the shoulder and hear her yell, "Ya don't gulp a mint julep, ya sip it—what the hell is the matter with you?") I love the old women who play the slot machines all day and tip well when they lose and better when they win. I enjoy the "flop," a Yahtzee-like dice game that involves taking a can full of the money of people who have done the flop and lost out from behind the register and letting people roll the dice to see if they will win.

I roam around the floor on days I am serving food, taking orders for fish fries, burger specials, wings. People annoy me, but not too much; I am mainly here on weekends now that I've remotely started my publishing job, and none of it is too much.

My boss is a woman named Eileen who has the permanently pursed lips of a lifetime cigarette smoker. She tells me a lot, laughing, when she's drinking at the bar, how much she loves me. I know, in the fashion of bars, she will not even remember me a year after I am gone.

■

On the corner of Madison Avenue, two blocks away from where I live and about ten minutes away from the pagan shop I've been going to AA at, there is a second pagan shop. I go in and ask the owner for Italian witchcraft books, but she only has Raven Grimassi's, which I have done enough research to know is not what I want, not yet, not until I have learned enough to tell truth and embellishment apart. I get a tarot reading. There is a person who is working that day, who, every time I come in after will ask me if I want a reading, and sometimes announce that there is a reader in the store to everyone while I am shopping. I think she believes I am very susceptible to the power of suggestion, but I ignore her more often than not. I know what I want. I know what I am looking for. Not expensive crystals and trinkets. Mostly, I buy herbs and candles.

■

The first reading I got at this second pagan shop on the street down the block from me was right around Valentine's Day. I'd been on a couple of dates with Gabe, who will later become a good friend, but who I will mostly lose touch with when I leave Cleveland, where we live down the street from one another. The reading I get that day will be about love, and the reader will get it all wrong. She will say there is a deep passion between me and a

Sagittarius (Gabe is a Sagittarius). I will fall for Gabe, but when I approach the idea of moving our few, movie-watching, kissing-on-my-front-porch-in-the-cold dates to something more, they will tell me they would rather be friends with me. Later, when I ask them why, they will say they just had a feeling we'd be friends for life, and also that they weren't ever going to leave Cleveland, and I was understandably hell-bent on getting out of it. They make weird little black-and-white films that, based in Cleveland as they are, remind me a lot of early Jarmusch stuff. Later, we made a short trans vampire film that I star in, based off one of my short stories.

This reading around Valentine's Day will turn out to be wrong, but the next time I go in and get one, a different woman from Romania reads with cards that aren't tarot. She gets a lot of things right. One of the things she says is that I've been leaning hard on the spirits to make a decision, but it's time to make it myself, it's time to jump in full force. Another thing she says is that there's a ring of sexual abusers around my rapist.

A few days later, I will walk onto a patio of a bar and hear a circle of my rapist's friends laughing about him exposing himself to people and I will flee Cleveland within a week for Philadelphia.

■

Every now and then, besides the pagan AA meeting I go to, I go to SMART Recovery meetings. Somewhere in them, I learn to think of the part of me that screams for self-destruction as a character in my head. I call him The Sadboy Narrator. He's a twelve-year-old mall goth in Hot Topic black clothes who has black emo-swoop hair and carries around *The Complete Works of Edgar Allan Poe* with him everywhere he goes. He's the one responsible for my dark spin on everything. Only the problem is, now that I have seen this little faux-vampire boy, I can't help but laugh about him all the time. The voice in my head that yells for destruction has been dropped off by his mom near the arcade to get some spiderweb combat boots to wear to middle school. It's ridiculous that I have been giving him so much room in my mind for so long.

Another exercise in SMART Recovery centers on a Rumi poem, "The Guest House." The poem goes:

> *This being human is a guest house.*
> *Every morning a new arrival.*
>
> *A joy, a depression, a meanness,*
> *some momentary awareness comes*
> *as an unexpected visitor.*
>
> *Welcome and entertain them all!*
> *Even if they're a crowd of sorrows,*
> *who violently sweep your house*
> *empty of its furniture,*
> *still, treat each guest honorably.*
> *He may be clearing you out*
> *for some new delight.*
>
> *The dark thought, the shame, the malice,*
> *meet them at the door laughing,*
> *and invite them in.*
>
> *Be grateful for whoever comes,*
> *because each has been sent*
> *as a guide from beyond.*

The idea behind the poem is that you greet, allow, and entertain your thoughts and emotions as they come through you, and you let them pass, rather than trying not to feel them, or to control them. I stop trying to control this Sadboy Narrator in my head. I even stop laughing at him. I let him talk. I let him mourn. And when he is finished, I say goodbye to him, and go along with my life without letting him be in control.

I am amazed by how well it works.

▪

One day, in the summer before the fall I go into the mental health crisis center, I walk into the bar that was across the street from the apartment I used to live in with the crumbling ceiling. There are a bunch of old guys at the bar, and they clap when I come in, surprising me. One of them, an artist and teacher of children who listens to The Jim Carroll Band's "People Who Died" a lot on the jukebox, says that they saw me in the *Cleveland Plain Dealer*, the article about my book bigger than the article about Playhouse Square's new season. I feel a little famous. I have one drink and leave, but I feel good.

Later, when I'm working at the Elks Lodge, I tell one of the regulars who gets me talking a lot that I'm a writer. He asks for my last name, googles me, and finds, immediately, a review in the *New York Times*. He tells everyone, even though I ask him not to say anything to anyone. I am a minor celebrity, suddenly, with people buying my book and asking me to sign it.

I think it's funny that I only feel famous in bars. It's not enough to make me want to start hanging out in them again, though. Not after what I've been through. Not after detoxing in a mental health crisis center, watching the world blank out into white as I had panic attacks I thought would kill me.

▪

I go to a bar down the street every few days to get lunch. I don't drink, except once in a while, and then only one. Mostly, I drink martinis with Gabe, just one, just enough to laugh and joke and loosen up. One night, me and Gabe go out to a bar, and I drink two drinks, and then I am saying I want drugs while Gabe is saying the two of us should go to a diner and have mozzarella sticks. I laugh.

"The difference between an addict and someone who is not an addict," I say.

Another night, Gabe calls me up a bit drunk and says he wants to do something wild. Knowing we have different definitions of wild, I suggest we find the house Screamin' Jay Hawkins grew up in and visit it. Gabe agrees enthusiastically and I spend an hour digging through census records to find the location. When I have found approximately where it is, I call Gabe, who says, "But I'm in my jammies now."

■

In my second reading at the pagan shop, the woman from Romania lays down cards and says I have to make my decision.

A few days later, I walk to the patio of the bar where I get lunch with a drink in my hand. My rapist's friends are there, talking about him. They laugh while they describe him showing his penis to people.

I make my decision. I quit the Elks Lodge. I rent a U-Haul. I have decided the time to get the fuck out is right now.

■

In the days that I am frantically trying to pack up my whole life, friends stop by. Larisse, one of the few people from my grad school who I really liked, brings me empty boxes and a going away card. "You didn't deserve any of this," she says. Paul and Amanda come by, helping me throw things into boxes and throw other things away. "I love Cleveland," Amanda says, "but Cleveland has not treated you well. You need to get out." Gabe comes by. He's going to miss me, he says, but he has also known this day was coming since the day we met.

Three days after I walk onto the bar patio where my rapist's friends are laughing about him showing his dick to people, my friend Mia comes on her motorcycle from Brooklyn. She accidentally leaves her phone charger at home, and somewhere near Cleveland, everyone who is following along with her trip on Google Maps (me, her partner, and our mutual friend Vivien) loses contact with her. Her partner texts me, worried. Vivien is not worried. I am—Cleveland is not friendly to trans people, and we lost touch with her when she was coming through the East Side, where there is allegedly at least one active serial killer working. When she gets back in touch, she is in a bar charging her phone, just fine. She rolls up to my apartment in Birdtown after night has fallen. The two of us sit on my porch and smoke cigarettes and drink iced tea. Most of my life is in boxes. I can't take it anymore.

We throw the rest of what's left into boxes, too. Mia sleeps in the hammock in my living room. My dog, Roxy Music, Dog of Doom, is so upset, convinced each time we leave the apartment that we are leaving her for good. Her barks are high-pitched and worried. I set up her kennel in the front seat of the U-Haul van I have rented.

The last thing we do before I leave the last apartment I live in in Cleveland for good is take the card <<redacted>> has signed out from under the frame it's been put behind. I rip his name and his words off the card. I draw a sigil for protection over it. I wrap it in black string. Me and Mia take it out to my backyard and bury it. We spit on the ground where it is buried and we both say "fuck you" to his name. It will be there for someone else to find, someday. I think about this person, innocently discovering my witchcraft, and I hope they understand that it wasn't for harm, but for my own protection. I hope they are not afraid, as I have been afraid for so long.

A NOVENA, A BLASPHEMY

DAY ONE

A Call to Prayer
by St. Hildegard of Bingen

We who have lost our sense and our senses—our touch,
our smell, our vision of who we are; we who frantically force and press
all things, without rest for body or spirit, hurting our
earth and injuring ourselves: we call a halt.

We want to rest. We need to rest and allow the earth to rest.
We need to reflect and to rediscover the mystery that lives in us, that is
the ground of every unique expression of life, the source of
the fascination that calls all things to communion.

We declare a Sabbath, a space of quiet: for simple
being and letting be; for recovering the great, forgotten truths;
for learning how to live again.

I can't say prayers to a God I'm not fully on board with, but
luckily for me, God has intercessors. I have acquired many of

them in my life as patrons: St. Alexis, the patron saint of the homeless; St. Francis of Assisi, the patron of my family, the DiFrancescos; St. Sebastian, the plague protector adopted by Catholic queers during the AIDS crisis who guards me through the COVID-19 crisis (along with my vaccinations). One day, when I cannot write and I think I will never be able to write again, I look up St. Hildegard of Bingen. She is the patron of artists, of writers, of composers, of those with vision. She suffered through her life with holy visions that she kept secret until they made her ill. It was only upon begging a higher-up in the church for permission to make her visions public that she began publishing her work. Her feast day, the day of her death, is the same day as my birthday.

I read the *Encyclopedia of Mystics, Saints & Sages* and learn that to successfully petition a saint, you must make offerings.

I lay in the hammock in my living room and I look up a nine-day prayer regimen to her on my smart phone. I say one of the prayers, which I don't believe all the words of, as it praises the God above her, and then, in my heart and in a quiet voice, staring at the ceiling, I begin to tell her of my problems. I am writing about trauma. I cannot find the form. I cannot finish projects. I have lost my vision, the thing which once sustained me as an artist. I used to be able to come to an idea and pursue it full force. Now, I lose confidence, I waffle, I give up. Please return my vision, St. Hildegard. In return, I promise to dedicate works to you.

I am a transgender degenerate, I often say, even though I don't fully believe it. None of us is one thing or another, and I am just as put together as I am falling apart. And yet, my prayers are earnest.

DAY TWO

A Prayer of Awareness
by St. Hildegard of Bingen

*Today we know of the energy that moves all things: the oneness
of existence, the diversity and uniqueness of every moment of creation,
every shape and form, the attraction, the allurement, the fascination
that all things have for one another.
Humbled by our knowledge, chastened by
surprising revelations, with awe and reverence
we come before the mystery of life.*

Italian Folk Magic tells me that saints and humans have
a reciprocal relationship. That we ask them for favors, and in
return we must build them shrines, make devotions to them,
learn about them. We must treat them like friends or lovers who
we want to know everything about. We must read their hagi-
ographies and figure out their favorite foods and what kind of
flowers they liked.

But Italians don't just beg and thank their saints, no, not at
all. They also punish them. If they do not grant the wishes of the
people who petition them, those people might take away their
altar, yell at them and curse them out, turn their icons so they
face the wall. Saints are bullied in Italian folk tradition, and why
not? How could someone so close to holy hear a prayer from the
depths of our heart, our truest wishes, our most sincere hopes,
and do nothing with their direct line to God?

I haven't tried direct petition of a saint before this, but something feels different even by day two. I don't think I'll be bullying
St. Hildegard, who was alleged to have been a lesbian, anyway,
an ancient member of the community, an ancestor. On day two,

I get a piece of feedback from the writer Sandra Lambert, who is acting as a beta reader for the collection, about the structure of the words I'm banging my head against, unable to finish, unable to put down, and uninspired to write anything besides. She says that memory comes in rising spirals. That when we recover the trauma that's happened to us, it repeats, but it gathers more and more detail as it does. She thinks this may be the structure I'm looking for.

And it is. I have petitioned St. Hildegard, yes, but I've also reached out to people, ones I know will help and assist me. If your car breaks down, pray to St. Christopher, but call your mechanic, too.

DAY THREE

"Creation is the song of God."
—St. Hildegard of Bingen

On the third day of my novena, I download the works of St. Hildegard and read them all morning, from the hammock in my living room. Her faith is astounding, her commitment to bringing new life to it inspiring. I imagine her hiding these words she wrote to breathe new life into scripture for most of her life, neither able nor willing to put herself at the center of them.

I download Scrivener, a piece of word processing software for long projects, and begin to play around with it. I am not the kind of person who can sit through a tutorial, no matter how long it takes me to figure things out on my own. I discover how I can color code notes to myself. I make a note in a different color for each repeating theme. And then, I go back and I stack them from brief mention, to heavier memory, to so much detail it hurt to recall. This is the way these memories came to me, asserting themselves to me, proving that nothing was right. And this is the way that I will tell them.

I look at the colors of the notes and highlights and think that I am weaving a tapestry. St. Hildegard was not a weaver, not that I know of, though St. Hildegard believed that the universe was woven of song.

DAY FOUR

A Prayer
by St. Hildegard of Bingen

Dare to declare who you are. It is not far from the shores of silence to the boundaries of speech. The path is not long, but the way is deep. You must not only walk there, you must be prepared to leap.

The book *Italian Magic: Secret Lives of Women* by Karyn Crisis tells me that the folk women of Italy who practiced magic prayed to the saints because "like helps like"—through a sense of identification. I cannot connect to many of the stories of saints: people who were beheaded, shot with arrows, torn apart by lions. But I can connect to St. Hildegard's vision. While I do not have visions in the technical sense, nor does the vision I do contain serve a God who lives in the clouds, I relate to the idea that something is so deeply felt and understood that it must be expressed. St. Hildegard's expressions of divinity were so pure, so beautiful, so fresh, and so, to use her own metaphor, green with growth. It occurs to me that what has been lacking in my life is not writing, which I still do in spurts and fits, but the sense of inspiration as a service to something else that can push me to create.

On the fourth day of my novena to St. Hildegard of Bingen, I write and I write, I compile, I see the form of where my project is going and work for hours in service to it. My vision has returned. I do not have to believe in the God that Hildegard believed in for this to happen. I just have to believe that I am working in the service of something greater than myself, which is what I have always believed about writing, anyway.

DAY FIVE

A Prayer
by St. Hildegard of Bingen

O leafy branch,
standing in your nobility
as the dawn breaks forth:
now rejoice and be glad
and deign to set us frail ones
free from evil habits
and stretch forth your hand
and lift us up.

Making time to pray to St. Hildegard before I go to work, I ask for her intercession. I ask that I am returned my vision. I ask that I am returned my ability to work towards this vision without compromise. All day, I sit at my desk in an office in Philadelphia. I sit and I work at the words of others, helping them hone their own visions. I come home, exhausted.

And, despite this exhaustion, there is something green and full of the possibility of growth that reaches me as I sit in front of my computer. So, on the fifth day of the novena, I write.

DAY SIX

St. Hildegard's Cookies of Joy Recipe

Ingredients:
12 tablespoons butter for mixture
1 tablespoon butter to grease cookie sheet
¾ cup brown sugar
⅓ cup honey
4 egg yolks
2 ½ cups spelt flour
1 teaspoon sea salt
2 rounded tablespoons spice that bring joy mix
(mix together equal parts Nutmeg, Cinnamon, Cloves)

Process: Melt the butter while mixing the sugar, salt, flour, and spice. Add honey and yolks to dry mixture and whisk. Add melted butter to mixture and continue whisking. Scoop tablespoon-sized balls of dough onto a greased baking pan and bake for around eight minutes at 400 °F.

On day six of my novena, I decide to make St. Hildegard's cookies of joy recipe. Recipes, in my way of thinking, are a way of honoring those who created them. Those people, people we love or respect or admire, used these recipes to sustain, to bring happiness to others. Recipes are a kind of spell, the best kind, I think.

The cookies have ground cloves, cinnamon, and nutmeg. I use my mortar and pestle to grind the spices together (except the nutmeg, which I do not have whole). Cloves, in magic, are for protection and clarity. Cinnamon is for protection and spirituality. Nutmeg, which can be hallucinogenic if overconsumed, is unsurprisingly for vision. It makes sense why St. Hildegard, an herbalist and natural healer, would use these spices in her special recipe. The cookies, with their warm spices, make me smile with joy. St. Hildegard was right.

I have also drawn a St. Hildegard for above my work desk. I'm not a visual artist, so it's crude and looks like it was done by a gifted child. Nevertheless, St. Hildegard watches over me as I work, as I write words, as I seek to find my vision again.

DAY SEVEN

A Prayer
by St. Hildegard of Bingen

Don't let yourself forget that God's grace rewards not only those who never slip, but also those who bend and fall. So sing! The song of rejoicing softens hard hearts. It makes tears of godly sorrow flow from them. Singing summons the Holy Spirit. Happy praises offered in simplicity and love lead the faithful to complete harmony, without discord. Don't stop singing.

Catholicism stresses its disbelief in superstition yet encourages such novenas. It is often said that one shouldn't expect a miracle. Yet miracles happen, they concede. I enjoy this sort of what if-ing, a healthy attitude towards that which can be seen and felt, with a door open just a crack for that which is inexplicable.

I am not a religious person, and the saints are not a stand-in for an all-knowing creator for me. They are deities unto themself (Catholics would revile this belief), and Hildegard, who was in touch with nature around her, whose work resonated with the concept of *veridas*, puts me in touch with something that the tradition I study does consider all-knowing: the mother of the Earth, the world around us, nature itself. When Hildegard painted a vision of Mary, she was not holding the baby Jesus, as she often is in representations, but a globe and a staff. The mother of the world. Nature. You cannot stop the leaves from swirling, the rain from falling. That is above and beyond what humans can do.

My search to tap into whatever muses or divinity I have lost is working. I am dedicated to creating something of the mess of essays and reflections I had before. I will shape it, I will, as a famous sculptor said, chip away the marble to find the angel. I will create something where there is nothing.

Perhaps I have been too wedded to my idea of myself as the creator of these things. Perhaps I haven't been giving the muses their due. Perhaps, with the intercession of Hildegard, I can change this.

DAY EIGHT

"Part of the terror is to take back our own listening,
to use our own voice, to see our own light."
—St. Hildegard of Bingen

Magic, for me, is deeply tied to ritual. I like this process of setting aside nine days' worth of time for prayer, for learning about the intercessor, for creating appropriate praise. I don't fool myself that this isn't blasphemy, in the eyes of the Church and probably the saint herself. Yet my intentions are true. I want to write a book that heals harm. I want to write a book about how far I've come in healing myself.

One night, losing my mind in a mental health crisis center, I asked a peer counselor how I had avoided death so often, how I had been through all the things I've been through in life—including being a missing person the FBI was looking for at one point—unscathed.

"Do you believe in God?" he boomed at me, a twelve-step believer to the core.

I stopped, shrugged, and with less theatrics than him and less than he might've imagined I would answer with, I said, "I guess so."

DAY NINE

"O moving force of Wisdom, you encircle the wheel of the cosmos, you encompass all that is, all that has life, in one vast circle."
—St. Hildegard of Bingen

I have spoken many words in these prayers, words that point to God as a heavenly Father and all-seeing, all-knowing sage. I don't know if I believe in God that way, and I don't have to. The saints I speak of, some related to me through their queerness, some related to me through profession, some related to me by name, some related to me by desperation, are enough. They bind and keep me and answer my prayers. They bring me back to my ancestors, who they interceded for as well. They give me faith in magic. Through mystical visions, the embracing of those unembraceable, through plague arrows, and the forgotten, they bind me to the understanding that magic is beyond our senses, in some special order of its own.

On the last day of the novena, I write.

A VICTORY

I am living in Philadelphia, in an old house with two floors, three bedrooms, a half-finished basement, and mice in the walls. My neighbors are an older couple with two dogs who I talk to in our adjoining backyards, and a family with a teenage boy who, one days, tells me his mom heard him calling me Alex, told him he should have more respect, and would like to know if I'd prefer to be called "Miss Alex" or "Mr. Alex." My heart breaks at the kindness of this young man who is sensitive to my gender identity and listens to his mom even when she's not around.

Around Thanksgiving, I am getting closer and closer to the mediation for the trial for the defamation case my rapist has brought against me. My brain shuts off. I am so stressed out I am no longer able to work. I am so stressed out my dog has picked up on my anxiety and developed a nervous tick, the flicking of her tongue out like a snake, repeatedly.

Fortunately, my publishing job has unlimited sick days, so this is not one of the times I will be fired for my poor mental health. But during the days I take off, things get bad. I lose the thread of reality, creating narratives about all the people who are out to get me. I do haphazard googling, spelling names wrong, convincing myself further. One day, when I am talking to my friend Vivien, I apologize for any way I may have hurt her and decide that suicide is the only way out (again). I take the broken glass from a picture frame that's fallen off my wall and hold it to the gently pulsing vein in my wrist. I stand there for some time, gently increasing the pressure. Then I drop the glass, begin crying until something like vomiting comes over my body. I don't puke, though, I just retch as if I'm trying to expel something from my being. After, I lay on my bed for a solid hour, unmoving, convinced I am dying and that my dog will probably eat my face when I do.

Finally, after a long time, I get cold and pull a blanket over me. This simple motion, one towards my comfort, breaks whatever state I am in. My mind slowly begins to recalibrate. I decide to up my dose of antipsychotic meds by half. I slowly begin to eat again, something I haven't done for days. I eat an English Muffin with butter and jam once a day for three days until I'm able to eat full meals again. My life comes back into line.

My friend Michelle calls me, worried, and asks about my plan for going to Cleveland for my defamation trial. I am taking a bus, I say, my best friend is picking me up at the bus station and taking me back the next day for the mediation. I am so scared, I tell her. Scared of a twelve-hour bus ride while my mind is in the state it is in, scared of the courtroom, scared that I will see my rapist now, after having not seen him for years. We slowly plan for all of it, on the phone. When I get off the call, I feel better.

I pack my suit jacket, a pair of black jeans, a button-down shirt, underwear, and socks in a bookbag. I pack a hat and scarf I've knitted for my nephew, a book for my best friend, a saddle bag for the moped I've given my niece, and a healing poppet I made for my best friend's husband, who has been unwell. I am as ready as I'll ever be.

The day before I'm to leave, my lawyer, Tyler, calls me. He asks if I'd like the good news or the not-so-good news first.

"The good, please," I say.

"The case has been dismissed. But I don't know if you can refund your flight."

I scream. I thank him. I cry a little.

"What happened?" I ask.

"His lawyer didn't say, exactly," Tyler says. "But I think he finally realized how poorly this whole thing was going to go for him. How much it would cost, and how he probably wasn't going to win."

I thank him again. I call everyone I know. My old lawyer from my activist days in New York, Ron, who has done way more than he had to for this case (convincing my lawyers to cut me a break on costs, sending a cease and desist letter to the predatory publisher who published the essay and then created lies about me to justify his actions when he capitulated to my rapist and printed a retraction), calls me up and we talk about what happened. He congratulates me on not giving up, sticking to my ideals, and winning.

"That's it!" I proclaim. "No more legal troubles!"

"Alex," he says, "how many times have we gotten off the phone with you saying that?"

We both laugh.

Other people thank me for what I have done. I feel like I've been in a war. I feel like I've been through hell. And I have. I think back to a few days before, the glass held against the tender skin above my pulse.

"I guess it was a game of chicken for him," I text my friend Vivien. "I said in the goddamn essay I never lose that game."

"You almost killed yourself," Vivien reminds me.

"Yeah, but that happens a lot when you play chicken. Part of the game," I type back.

"Just what I love about you," she deadpans by text. "Your unshakable cool."

For a few weeks after, I google my rapist's name every day again, to make sure he hasn't killed himself. He hasn't. I think about the life he's living now. From what I heard on the patio of the bar that day, from his friends, it's unchanged. But I also know that the next time someone reports his behavior, there is a record of his being investigated for rape, and he will likely go to prison. It's not much. It's not the same as getting him off the streets. But it's the most I can do.

I think about my feelings about the whole situation for a long time. I am angry and hurt, but not in the ways I used to be, where no one around me was spared from these feelings. They are more of a dull ache inside me. I miss the time when <<redacted>> and I were friends, before this war began, even though our friendship was predicated on things that were harmful to us both. I feel the ache of loss over my life years ago, as imperfect as it was, and all the people who were collateral damage in this battle. I feel shame and embarrassment over the last year, when I've been publicly fundraising for the legal case, when people have set up burner accounts on social media to tell me how I'm just looking for attention, how I'm lying about the rape. I know it's not true, and I wonder how many other people think it, anyway. Mostly, I feel overwhelmingly elated that the whole thing is over; my happiness and lightness feel like being released from heavy chains. I touch the edges of my longtime death wish, still there, still razor-sharp, but now I put it down before it cuts too deep. And, finally, I decide that I forgive <<redacted>> for everything: not because he deserves it, but because holding onto it would only harm me, not him.

Forgiveness is something I learned a lot about in ancestor veneration. In the book *Honoring Your Ancestors* by Mallorie Vaudoise, there is a chapter that describes healing ancestral trauma. In it, she says, "forgiveness doesn't happen because the person who hurt you deserves it. It happens because you deserve it. You deserve peace. You deserve to have space in your life for new, beautiful things, and the energy to make them happen." There were a lot of things I had to forgive my ancestors for, particularly my father. He is my most recently deceased ancestor, and in Southern Italy it is believed, much like the Catholic concept of purgatory, that such ancestors must cross a bridge covered in the blades of knives, needles, and thorns to progress to an afterlife beyond. In learning to forgive my father for the things he did in this life, I also learned to forgive the reasons I've always been attracted to self-destruction. There has been a deep trauma that's run through my life that he was not the source of—that probably started long before him—but that I can help heal through helping him cross the bridge of the afterlife through my forgiveness. Letting go of these traumas, both the ancestral ones and the ones that are a part of my own experience on this earth, is for me as much as it is for anyone else, probably even more so.

In both cases of forgiveness, I feel a kind of relief. A letting go. A severing of a cord that had held me tight to the things that would destroy me.

■

A few weeks after this victory, the winter solstice comes. It is the longest night of the year, after which the days become longer and the nights shorter. But instead of a day where darkness reigns, it is considered the day of the triumphant return of the sun, which cannot be extinguished, which, no matter how long the darkness gets, still comes back to us. I wake up around 2 a.m. that night, and I light candles and place them around my kitchen so that, as I make my coffee, as I wake up, they are there to light my way. As I am drinking my coffee, I sit down and write all the darkness of the year that has passed, much of which has been written about here. I write about my suicidal ideation, my temper, my loss of friends, my betrayal by friends, about caring for those who cannot or will not care back. I write it all, and beneath it, I write a prayer to the light, about how it is undefeatable, how it may wait but always returns to dispel the darkness. Then, carefully, I take a candle and walk to my herb cabinet where I remove rose petals, dried flowers from my friend Christina's garden that smell like summer, mint, and rue. I wrap them carefully in the paper I have just written on and repeat the prayer. Then, I burn the paper and the herbs in my offering bowl.

I sit in the darkness with the dim light of candles all around me. The darkness is deep and it is long, but soon, soon the sun will shine again. I will be waiting to welcome it.

PRAYER AT THE SHRINE OF ST. RITA IN PHILADELPHIA

Saint Rita, Margherita, daughter of peacemakers, mother of violent sons, forgiver. St. Rita, to whom the shrine sits in the city I come to rest in. St. Rita, did you draw me here? Pearl of Roccaporena, what can you forgive? White bees went in and out of your mouth after your baptism, St. Rita, and I can't pretend to know what that means. Your parents assumed you were blessed, but what do mortals know of heaven's designs? Was your prayer a monkey's paw, St. Rita? Did you sacrifice your sons for the forgiveness of their father's killer? St. Rita, can you forgive me calling the police, the arm of state violence? Can you forgive me screaming threats? St. Rita, can you forgive him the blood that ran from my body?

You birthed your first son at the age of twelve, St. Rita. What did you know of love, or what did you know of persecution? I assume the latter, as do many historians. Was there a moment, St. Rita, when you rejoiced in his death? Even if you didn't tell anyone, you could tell me, St. Rita, and I would understand.

St. Rita, when the thorn of the crown of Jesus entered your forehead, did you orgasm? I will forgive you if you did, as if you need my forgiveness. Your wound never healed, true stigmata.

I still don't let my lovers touch certain parts of my body. Some wounds never heal, St. Rita.

The bells pealed at your death, St. Rita, but don't you grow tired of it, you saints, the bells pealing without human hands? Don't you grow tired of your miracles, the sick healed and the lame made whole? Don't you wish for a world where they did not have these wishes? Does the perfume that rises from your corpse ever begin to sicken you? Don't you hear the same old, bitter song over and over? "Heal me, St. Rita. Heal the person who broke me."

Your devotees carry red roses, St. Rita. They are said to have bloomed for you in the winter, just before you died. These old women, carrying bouquets. What have they endured? I come with a single red rose to your shrine. Your statue stands in a place of honor with lit candles all around it. You hold the thorn from Jesus's crown. A young man is there, and though I do not know what he has endured, we circle you from opposite sides. I write words on a plain white sheet next to the basket at your feet. I see the words of others here and there, partially obscured by the folds of paper. "Alzheimer's" and "abuse" and words in Latin. I write my prayer to you, St. Rita. St. Rita, will you listen? In the reliquary, saints' statues' hands are threaded with white papers. A relic of St. Kateri Tekakwitha is there. I greet the saints I know: St. Anthony of Padua, St. Jude, St. Therese, Michael the Archangel. The feeling of hope and desperation hangs in the air. All these prayers, St. Rita, where do they go when you have seen them? Can you see them all? Will you intercede?

They say your body remained incorrupt for hundreds of years, St. Rita, but was finally destroyed by "natural forces." My body grows older every day, a new pain, a mark on my skin where there was none before. The cloth that touched your dead body is a holy relic, enshrined in glass in the walkway. Can you transfer holiness through touch, St. Rita, or do we capitalize on your blessed form?

Is a single red rose enough, St. Rita? It is the same color as my blood. I hope you will forgive me, St. Rita, for my lack of forgiveness. I hope you will forgive him for his vengeance. I hope your magnanimity will spread like wildflowers, over both of us and everyone in between. I come to you as we all do, St. Rita, with prayers and offerings and a hope. Perhaps it is hope that is holy, that we be better than ourselves, that we borrow your grace as our own. Perhaps even the boy who circled your statue as I did wishes for that kind of holiness. Can you make him a good boy, St. Rita, the kind who would never behave as your husband or your sons did? Can you smite him if he does, St. Rita? I am only asking. I am merely asking.

ANCESTORS

When I move to Philadelphia, I set up an altar to my ancestors. I cover a folding table with a yellow cloth and, because I don't have pictures of most of them, write their names and the dates of their birth and death on blue cards that I tape to the wall above it. I go back four generations, to people who I have no concept of at all. I hang a cimaruta pendant between them. Next to my father's name, I tape the one picture I have of him: a Polaroid from when he won the Diet Pepsi taste test in our local supermarket in the early '90s. In the picture, he stands next to cardboard cut outs of Ray Charles and the Ray Charles singers, looking amused. I have always kept this picture because I know how amused he would be by the fact that it's the only one I have of him. Underneath his name, I tape another Polaroid, this one an old, grainy one from a camera and pack of ancient film I bought in a thrift store. This picture has my blood niece, Scarlet, and I sitting in my old kitchen in Queens, laughing. I leave space under the youngest generation, because in Italian tradition, you leave space for generations to come. I don't think I'll be having children, but my niece may want to one day, and I don't want to ruin that for her, even accidentally.

I put offerings on the table: bread and Montepulciano, a white candle. I light the candle and pour myself a glass of wine to drink with them. I can feel their calm presence, their gratitude for remembrance. I also have my Sicilian playing cards out so I can speak to them.

■

I do some research on the places my ancestors came from. I search out topographical maps of Calabria and Sicily and Abruzzo on Amazon and put them in my cart, along with a hammered copper offering bowl which I plan to use for the limoncello I've decided I'll make for them. Limoncello, it turns out, is simple to make: something, like ricotta cheese, that seems daunting until you actually look it up and see it requires very few steps and almost anyone could do it. You peel ten lemons and put them in a glass quart container, then pour a liter of 80 to 100 proof vodka over them. You let them sit for at least four days, or up to thirty. Then, you strain the lemon peels out, pour in a cup of simple syrup, and chill. I plan to offer this to them on their birthdays throughout the year. I also order a bunch of PAYDAY candy bars, my dad's favorite, which an old radio blog by someone who knew him in his DJ days tells me he would eat every day at lunch until he began to worry that the caramel and nuts would stick in his teeth even after brushing and affect his delivery.

To venerate our ancestors, we must learn what they liked. I don't know much about my ancestors except where they came from, so I spend some time searching the liqueurs of Sicily and Calabria. I spend some time thinking about items they might want, like a crucifix or saint medals.

■

In Southern Italian folk tradition, you read fortunes through the regional playing cards of the area your family is from. Though my family is from Calabria, Abruzzo, and Sicily, the Sicilian playing cards are the easiest to find, so I go with that region. There are four suits, just like in a regular deck of playing cards, but in this deck, it is swords, clubs, coins, and cups. The traditional method for reading these cards is three lines of three cards each, the first to tell what matter the cards are speaking about, the second to tell what is influencing the matter, and the last to tell the outcome. They are a lot like reading tarot cards but, being closer to my family's tradition, I find that these read very clearly for me whenever I read from them, though I am also a tarot reader.

■

As I sit at the altar, drinking the Montepulciano, I stare into the candle flame. Some people, when they do candle magic or ancestor worship, see visions in the flame. I transfer my eyes from the flame to the picture of my dad. At first, the bright spot from the candle in my vision obliterates his face entirely. Then, as it fades, I can also see my dad's face moving, animated. It is such a comfort. I have not seen him alive in motion for twenty-two years now. He is speaking in the vision. He is trying to tell me something. I pick up my Sicilian playing cards.

■

My dad was a radio DJ for most of his life. I've spent a lot of times on message boards and Facebook groups that are for the purpose of remembering the radio stations he worked for, looking for anyone who remembers him. I've found very little. I spent a while looking for the tapes from his old radio stations, but most, it seems, were destroyed when Hurricane Agnes hit and flooded Wilkes-Barre and the surrounding areas. I have spent a lot of time looking for his voice, which I can still, barely, hear in my mind.

My dad was a first-generation child of immigrants from Italy. He was tall and olive-skinned and dark-haired. He loved baseball and basketball. As I think these things, I think of items I might put on my altar for him. A cigarette, a baseball card, a picture of Frank Sinatra.

My dad had a horrible temper. I think he inherited it from his father, a man I never met. I think he grew up in an abusive environment, and, knowing nothing else, created one for his family, too. His temper, which you could see he was about to give in to when he bit his tongue between his teeth, was violent. For a long time, when I was young, my mom would warn me against feeling anger because it could come out like my father's. In effect, I learned to hide my feelings, to push them down, to pretend they didn't exist. Now, when I feel my anger, it scares me. It reminds me of my dad's.

When we do ancestor work, we don't just venerate. We call on the good parts of our ancestors and ask them to help us understand the bad parts, too, the generational traumas that are passed down to us intact if we do nothing to change them. I am working so hard to change them.

■

The first card I draw from my deck is the Five of Swords: regret. My dad is sorry for so much. I'm flooded with memories: lousy ones like the time he pulled my niece's hair when she was four, and happy ones like the time when she was an infant and I watched him watch her sleep with awe and adoration on his face. I know he wanted to be a good father and grandfather. I know he tried so hard.

"I forgive you, Dad," I say. But when I look up, the light from the candle burned into my retina still makes him look like he's talking. So I pull another card. This card deals with a last will and testament. I think about how my dad had planned to sell the house he bought and paid for after I, his youngest kid, moved out of it, and how that plan was thwarted when he fell ill and my mom got power of attorney over him. She used to taunt him about it. My mom, before she got sick, made a point to tell me that in her will, her kids would get everything equally—except if one of us wanted to live in her house, and then the others would not be able to sell it. Effectively, this meant she was giving her house to my brother, who had lived there his whole life, never moving out, without feeling bad about slighting her other children. I can see how angry this makes my dad. He's worried about me, that what he worked his whole life to provide for me amounted to nothing, that I'm struggling to get by like I always do.

"It's okay, Dad," I say. "I'm okay."

■

I was already well into my study of Italian witchcraft when I obtained my first set of Sicilian playing cards. When it was time to bless them, I had a bowl of pink Himalayan sea salt all ready to bury them in under the new moon. It is the same salt I use when someone I don't like comes into my house and I throw it over every place they've been and sweep it out the back door when they leave. I know these things sound superstitious and a little silly, but these small acts connect me to the people I came from and dispel a myth that many of us live with, that I lived with for so long, that we are alone in the world. I am not alone, despite being estranged from my living family. I have generations of people watching over me. My actions, now that I've connected to them, are not just for me alone, but for many people who want what's best for me. When I read my cards, when I use my sea salt for cleansing, when I do any number of little things they may or may not have done, I can feel them somewhere inside me that I don't fully understand, but that I also can't deny.

■

I call on my grandmother when I cook, and when I read my cards. I call on her even though I never knew her in real life. I call on her because I know she would want to guide me, if I let her. I want to let her.

I learned how to make an Italian American Sunday gravy for her. I learned to cook lentils with bacon (as a substitute for pig's feet) on New Year's Day for prosperity in the new year. I am making the limoncello instead of buying it, for her. I call on her when my kitchen gets too dirty, and I don't have the strength or the will to clean it. I know that she loves these moments, because I know she dreamed of her grandchildren, and I know those dreams included me. I can feel her joy when I call on her, after so many years of not knowing her at all.

My grandmother, Assuntina, was twenty-one and both of her parents were dead when she married my grandfather. My grandfather, Antonio, came here from Naples on a ship through Ellis Island in 1913, when he was nineteen. He was born in Farindola, in the Abruzzo region of Italy. I try to imagine them. I go on Google Street View and look at the cobblestone streets of Farindola, the tan buildings with balconies that preside over those crowded streets. I look at the cliffside houses of Cantanzaro, where my grandmother was from, its opulent churches, its fountains and statues. I picture a teenage Antonio and a baby Assunta walking through these streets, streets they would never see again in their lives. I imagine all the twists and turns life took to put them together when he was a thirty-two-year-old coal miner, and she was a parentless twenty-one-year-old woman in Hazleton, Pennsylvania. I think of Hazleton, too, what a far cry it was from the beautiful places of their youth. I look at their shared gravestone on a memorial site, which has a carving of the Pieta on it. I think, perhaps, I will buy a little Pieta for their altar.

I know all these facts about my grandparents from the website familysearch.org, where my blood niece has spent the last several years piecing together marriage licenses, death certificates, obituaries, and other documents to compile our family history. I find it all when I'm idly looking, like I do sometimes. I have never been able to compile our family history as far and in as detailed a manner as my niece has. She is the reason that, on my altar, I go four generations back. She started researching them around the time she stopped speaking to me because we got in an argument over politics. It's been about four years since we've talked. She doesn't answer my text messages. But she has done this thing—create a public family tree—that is a gift to me I may never be able to tell her about.

■

My dad's response to me is troubled, and I say a short prayer for him, that he make it over the fraught bridge between life and the afterlife. I pull a card to see what my grandmother has to say. It is the Five of Cups: a card of abundance.

"See, Dad?" I laugh, the wine and the candlelight making me suddenly warm. "Listen to your mother. I have all I need."

■

I know my ancestors were flawed people. I know there are traumas that run through my bloodline, like everyone has. But when I call on my ancestors for their wisdom, for their kindness, for their cooking help, I call on the best parts of them. These parts strengthen each time they are called upon. They help my intuition, they help guide me. Sometimes they are in my dreams. My dreams have been more and more vivid since building the altar, though I usually only remember my nightmares that wake me up in the midst of them. The more I venerate the parts of them that were strong, kind, and wise, the more the curses of anger and human failings fall away from them. They are light. They are parts of me, all reaching through time, to give me the best that they can, now that human living does not keep them from doing so.

■

I pull a playing card for my grandfather, Antonio, to speak through, and it is the Three of Coins: he's worried about how I deal with money. I think about him, a poor coal miner, and I understand the worry. I promise I will take it under consideration in the future.

The magical thing that happens when I pull this card, though, is that I can hear all of my ancestors giving me different messages, all of which are right. I can hear their warm bickering in their heavy Italian accents. I can feel their care for me, which comes out in this disagreement. Each of them want for me, from their own experience and perspective, what is best. They are so happy to be called upon together, to have this moment of warm familial misunderstanding, all of them right in their own way.

■

Normally, I might be confused by all these contradicting messages from the cards. But I see them all as true, all as my own contradictions and warring desires and all the messy, imperfect things that make me human, just as I venerate the people who I know carried good and bad thoughts and feelings and actions in them, as well. The messages that contradict each other remind me of what it means to be human, to, to, as Whitman said, contain the multitudes we all carry within us, which are as wide as the oceans my ancestors crossed over to get here, to bring me to this spot I sit in today. They were people—they are *my* people—and each thing they tell me is true, in its own way. My grandmother is right that I have everything I could dream of, that I am the wildest of her own dreams and my abundance is clear. My father is right about the unfairness of estranged family. My grandfather is right, too: I may have all I need, but it never hurts to make a buffer for the future, for rainy days. I listen to them in ways that I might not if they were alive, if they were speaking to me out loud instead of through these cards. I, who am so headstrong I barely listen to anyone, sometimes need magic to hear simple voices that speak with love as clearly as I do now.

■

In my kitchen, after I speak to them all, I begin peeling lemons. When I bought the Montepulciano today, I bought vodka as well. I peel the bright citrus, its sting burning the little cut places on my hands, and put it all into an airtight container with the vodka. I sit it on my shelf in my kitchen to wait. I am making something for them, these people who have made me. They are waiting, somewhere in a world beyond where I can see, to drink it with joy, to argue into the night around the table, to send me the best they have, which may not be the best thing in the world, but which is mine alone, the best for me.

BREAKING THE CURSE

Spell for Binding

Take something he has left behind.
Wrap it tightly with string, using all of your desire for healing and some
of your anger.
Put it in a box.
Put it in your closet.
Try to put it out of your mind.

While I am in the mental health crisis center, the group I am in writes down areas we want to improve in our lives. I end up, after much thought, with "spirituality" and "relationships." I read about southern Italian folk traditions. One of the key tenets of this tradition is to keep your kitchen immaculate. It is the job of generations of peasant women. There are no special tools or trinkets or amulets needed, nothing other than what you would have in your kitchen if you cared deeply about your kitchen.

While I am in the crisis center, unbeknownst to me, my next-door neighbor, Dani, cleans my kitchen as best she can. I know how much pain she is in regularly, and I know how she never cleans her own kitchen. It is a gift of friendship. When I leave the crisis center one night for the ER, leave the ER, and walk across the western suburbs of Cleveland to return to my home in the middle of the night, sure I am dying, I come home and find my knives laid out and gleaming on towels on the kitchen table. When I see this, the first thing I do is run to the closet I keep a magic spell in to make sure it is not gone.

■

My first act of magic was a binding spell. Someone who had hurt me left something behind in my home, and I bound it in acrylic cord, wrapped it in a bag, put it in a shoebox, and kept it in my closet for over a year.

I do not like that my first act of magic had a bit of darkness to it, and I cannot say how well it worked. I can say that my nonmagical actions around this event likely prevented it from happening to someone else.

■

Spell for Ancestors

Take pictures of your ancestors and put them on your kitchen table.
Burn a dollar bill for each of them, so they have currency in the afterlife.
Wish them well in their journeys.

After I return home from the crisis center, I decide to spend some of my dwindling money on a genetic test. I spit into a tube, send it off, and wait. While I wait, I think of all the things I might learn. Maybe my family is not my family. This seems unlikely.

What I do find is that I'm exactly what I've always been told I am: split nearly down the middle between Polish and Italian ancestry. The Italian ancestry is a bit stronger, and where exactly it comes from is broken down regionally. The Calabrian heritage is no surprise, with my olive skin, the nearly black hair on my head, and my propensity for growing body hair. What this test tells me that I didn't know is that my ancestors are from Sicily, a region that the Italian folk traditions I'm studying were strong in.

■

One day, in the crisis center, when my new antidepressant is beginning to kick in, I call my best friend and say, "It feels like the curse is broken."

I am in Cleveland. In Cleveland, "the curse" refers to their sports teams' long-standing inability to win a championship.

■

Spell for Protection

Put garlic, rue, black peppercorns, sea salt, and a chili pepper in olive oil.
Seal the container and leave in a dark place.
Shake once a day for a month.
Use the oil to make the sign of a cross on each entrance to your house.

When I get home, even though Dani has cleaned my kitchen, I decide to clean it deeper, in the method of Italian folk traditions. I remove everything from my kitchen. I wipe down all the shelves, all the walls, I clean out the refrigerator, I scrub the floors. I wipe everything I took out and bring it back. I sprinkle sea salt in the corners, sweep it to the center and out the door. While I do all this, I boil a large pot of water with a lemon cut in half, star anise, cloves, cinnamon, and sea salt in it. When the kitchen is clean, you save the water from the pot as a purification liquid you can spray around to clear any air that needs it.

I buy a little dish for salt at a gift shop. It's hand-thrown on a kiln. I go to a church rummage sale and buy a heavy gold-leafed dish with a "Made in China" stamp on the bottom; it's to keep fruit in, which, for me, symbolizes abundance. I go on Etsy and buy a print of the patron saint of bakers, St. Honoré, which I hang above my stove. My neighbor Tesh gives me wooden kitchen witch spoons for my birthday, the most innocuous of which I hang above my sink.

Everything is gleaming.

A few weeks later, when I relapse on alcohol and benzos, I look around the disaster in my kitchen and wonder how I will ever clean it again.

■

I start going to an outpatient rehab. A group of us sit in a room and talk with a therapist present. When the talk comes and stays on spirituality one day, a few weeks in, I listen to everyone talk about how into it they are, and use general terms, or other people's traditions they've heard about. There is a "spark of energy," there is "the universe," there is "God as I know Him." At first, I join the conversation enthusiastically. Eventually, when I realize we are talking generalized bullshit we pretend to be experts on, I get quiet.

We move onto a section of rehab about sex, relationships, and addiction. During this section, somewhere, I start talking about the person who hurt me, who left the item I did a binding spell on in my apartment. I don't say his name, even though it comes up in my head a lot. I don't say much of what he did to hurt me, referring to it as "the assault." What I do say is that I found a way to release this trauma, which is true. And that it was superpersonal, but it had great meaning to me. I am talking about ritual in the most general terms I can.

The woman who runs the group stops and looks at me and says, "That sounds beautiful. I'm glad you had that. I wish that for everyone."

Group ends early.

■

Spell for Cleansing Your Bed

Throw sea salt on every piece of him that is left from sleeping there.
Sweep it onto the floor.
Sweep it through the kitchen.
Sweep it through the front door.

I decide I don't care if kitchen magic is magic, because if I follow the Italian folk traditions, I have a really clean kitchen more often than not. This is something I've struggled with throughout life: cleaning up my own messes.

■

In Italian folk tradition, you don't judge people who put the evil eye on others intentionally. You don't judge these women, because, according to them, you never know what someone has done.

■

I started seeing a trauma therapist two years ago when a dog mauled me as I was walking down the street. The name of the street I got mauled by a dog on was also the name of the man who assaulted me. Maybe that's a coincidence. My doctor recommends a therapist, and I go.

I see him for a while, then feel better. So, I stop going.

Two years later, when I have health insurance again, I start seeing this same therapist again. He calls my trauma a "CVS receipt," and also tells me that I have to look at what I'm gaining by holding onto it. This doesn't make any sense at all, to me. Of course, I don't want to hold onto it. I also have no idea how to let it go.

■

Ritual Bath for Ridding Yourself of Negative Energy

Draw yourself a bath and fill it with sea salt, lemon peel, rue, and Florida water.
Light candles on the edge of the tub.
Wash yourself from head to foot with the intention of ridding yourself of the energy.
Put out the candles with water from the tub.
Dry your body from head to foot.

Rehab, after the crisis center, works like magic, and by that I do not mean that I snap my fingers, and everything is okay. I mean that I keep practicing doing the right thing for myself, and what I work for happens.

■

By the time I go to the crisis center, I have been trying to get help for two years. Two years of failed attempts at therapy. Two years of being told I'm doing the therapist's job better than them. Two years of being told I sound like I have everything processed and am really together. I am a convincing talker, I suppose.

In the crisis center, I smoke cigarettes on a porch with a butterfly bush planted in front of it. Hummingbirds dart through the air. The pillows are plastic. There is a stack of outsider art by the spent markers in the craft corner. I take some markers and draw something like the evil eye in bright colors. It looks radioactive. I write *"sá benedica"* above it. Outside, on the streets of Cleveland, a car accident happens and a man with a gun chases away the person driving the car who caused it. Drug altercations happen; strung out women beg while dealers laugh. Sex workers wait at the bus stop to step into someone's car.

One night, I wake up and imagine someone is ready to shoot me from the outside my window. I throw myself into the hallway, bruising my toe, my knees. I have a panic attack and end up in the hospital.

One afternoon, when someone asks me about the problems in my life, I say, among other things, my writing career is blossoming. The person writing my words down says, "That's a problem?"

■

The weekend I relapse, after I start outpatient rehab, is my friend's thirtieth birthday weekend. I decide to make pastries. I have been snorting benzos for two days. I make a tart with a chocolate sable crust, goat cheese mousse with chocolate chips in it, topped with strawberries and pomegranate; I make a key lime pie that says "Dirty 30" in toasted meringue; I make cake-cookies with lemon curd between the layers and raspberries on top.

Before I start to make them, before I black out for the night and forget most of it, I call on my Nonna Assunta, who I have never met in real life, to make sure they all come out well.

And they do. The pastries are great, and everyone enjoys them. I am a mess.

A few days later, at rehab, I break down, saying, "No one thinks I have problems, but I'm a trainwreck, I'm a trash fire."

Within a few weeks, I don't call myself words like this anymore.

■

Spell for Blessing Tarot Cards

Get to know the figures in your deck.
Look for them in the world around you.
When you have seen some of them, sit down with your cards
and light a cigarette.
Pull a few cards at random.
Blow smoke on each card, and in greeting, say, "I remember you."

I have nightmares for a long time after being assaulted. They wake me up into panic attacks often.

Some nights I have dreams about the person who hurt me healing and me giving the item he left behind back.

■

I tell my best friend, who has known me since childhood, who knew my family, about my genetic test. I am exactly who I have always been told I am, I say, somewhat disappointed. No family secrets, no surprises. The crazy people who raised me are my people, no doubt.

"You're the perfect combination of your mother and father," she says. "You're a stunning artist, like your mom, and you are charming as hell, like your dad. You're a once-in-a-lifetime product of generations of people who loved you, even if they weren't perfect."

I think of all these generations of people, doing their best. I think of the ship record I once found on an ancestry site that marked my Nonna Assunta's passage to the New World. I think of my Gram, Helen, who helped raise me, how fiercely loving she was to the people who mattered to her, how casually cruel she could be to the people who did not. I think of my mother's neurosis, which I have inherited, but also how she drew and painted wonderfully as a child, a talent that was subverted into making clothes and Halloween costumes for her family once she was married. I think of my dad, his dark hair, olive skin, and eyes the same shade of pastel green as mine; how everyone loved him for his humor and easy nature, and how bad his temper was, too—both things I can see in myself.

I am exactly who all these people wanted me to be. They are woven into me. I am all of them, and also myself. I make a promise to be the best version I can of that self, to honor all of them.

And the curse is broken.

■

Spell for Growth and Healing

On the vernal equinox, get a flowerpot, potting soil, seeds,
a piece of paper, and a pen.
On the paper, write all the good things you wish to draw into your life,
and place them at the bottom of the flowerpot.
Plant the seeds.
Every time you water the seeds, you water your intentions.
As the plants grow, as you tend and care for them, so you tend and care
for the goodness that you are drawing into your life.

About the item the man who assaulted me left behind:

It was a handkerchief, monogrammed, cotton. I wrapped it up in acrylic yarn with all my anger, with all my desire to keep him from hurting others. I put it in a bag. I put it in a box. I put it in my closet. There it stayed for over a year.

One day, when I am in rehab, I take it out of the closet. Before I know what I am doing, I unwind it. There are knots and tangles in the yarn, and I can feel my anger in them as I undo them.

I take the handkerchief out to my backyard. I also take a pewter dish a powerful witch has given me, my lighter, a eucalyptus smoke cleansing stick.

In the pewter dish, I light the handkerchief on fire. The air feeds it while I burn the eucalyptus stick and circle its smoke around me. Fire purifies. Smoke cleanses.

When the handkerchief has burned nearly all the way out, I put out the embers with wet leaves and earth. I take the dish inside and wash the remaining burned areas with water.

I walk back into my kitchen and begin to do my dishes.

(Use this blank space to create some sort of magic—even if it only makes sense to you.)

EPILOGUE

"Among all people, enlightenment bears the same characteristics, whatever the cultural interpretations through mythology, doctrine, psychological theory, etc. Enlightenment is an experience, not an idea. The person feels struck by a burst of light . . . Suddenly the world is seen or felt, as spiritual and eternal, rather than the day to day existence of drudgery and confusion. The person feels totally alive with a childlike joy that, in fact, most children probably never know, for the sunstruck person has gone beyond the child's fear of darkness by traveling through it."

—RACHEL POLLACK, *Seventy-Eight Degrees of Wisdom:*
A Tarot Journey to Self-Awareness

BELIEF

There is no reason to engage with magic if you don't believe you'll live. There is no reason to connect to your ancestors, to call on the spirits, to pray to the saints, if you are ready to end everything. To believe in magic is to believe in life—your own, those who have come before you—to believe in existence. The act of magic is an act of healing and the belief in your ability to heal is magical in and of itself.

You can't believe in anything if you don't believe you will live. There is no reason to draw a ritual bath, to make a magical potion, to grow seeds if you don't believe you will be there to see the outcome. To believe in magic is to believe in a future, no matter how far or hazy it seems. To believe in magic is to take steps towards living.

For decades, I believed there was no saving me. *Trauma changes the brain*, was a common claim I saw. *The brain after prolonged trauma becomes hardwired differently, to be in a constant state of fight or flight.* These were things I believed were true.

But the traumatized brain can heal. It can create new pathways. There is a certain measure of faith you have to have for it to do so. It doesn't matter what the faith is in, just that it is there.

■

In his 2019 article on BBC called "Do humans have a 'religion instinct'?" Brandon Ambrosino writes about Andrew Newberg, a neuroscientist who looks at exactly what happens to the human brain when focused on religious ritual:

> . . . *the parietal lobe, located in the upper back part of the cortex, is the area that processes sensory information, helps us create a sense of self, and helps to establish spatial relationships between that self and the rest of the world, says Newberg. Interestingly, he's observed a deactivation of the parietal lobe during certain ritual activities.*
>
> *"When you begin to do some kind of practice like ritual, over time that area of brain appears to shut down," he said. "As it starts to quiet down, since it normally helps to create sense of self, that sense of self starts blur, and the boundaries between self and other—another person, another group, God, the universe, whatever it is you feel connected to—the boundary between those begins to dissipate and you feel one with it."*
>
> *The other part of the brain heavily involved in religious experience is the frontal lobe, which normally helps us to focus our attention and concentrate on things, says Newberg. "When that area shuts down, it could theoretically be experienced as a kind of loss of willful activity—that we're no longer making something happen but it's happening to us."*

In the article, other scientists talk about early rituals as a sort of bonding practice for nomadic humans when they began to, bluntly put, annoy the shit out of each other. A ritual dance would be called, and, likely through the two parts of the brain described by Newberg, the group would again feel at peace with each other, having experienced something as a unit that felt inexplicable and holy. In this way, when I do magic, when I worship my ancestors, the part of me that is just me disappears, and I am connected to something larger than myself, something I must survive to honor.

In a 2010 NPR article titled "Is Believing in God Evolutionarily Advantageous?" researchers set up an experiment in which children are introduced to a game they can't win without cheating, then placed in three groups: one unsupervised, one told they are supervised by a supernatural presence, and one supervised by scientists. The surprise results were that the children "supervised" by the supernatural presence cheated as little as the group supervised by scientists. The scientists believe that a large part of why humans so overwhelmingly evolved into spiritual beings is that belief in God or gods creates a sense of order in which we self-regulate our actions to be moral and advantageous towards the whole rather than self-motivated. The American Psychological Association, in an article called "A Reason to Believe," mirrors this claim, adding that belief in God created greater social cohesion necessary for modern life.

These are all fine reasons why religion might exist and endure, and even create a sense of peace and cohesion and love for one's fellow man greater than we might be able to without it. But it's hard to deny how many wars, how many acts of atrocity, and how much dehumanization the concept of religion has caused in the world. One could find proof of this all over the world, but perhaps the most horrific example is the mass graves full of children recently found around church-run assimilation schools for Indigenous children in Canada and the US.

This is where we get into the sticky part of religion. Believing in an invisible presence that guides us towards greater humanity may well be something all humans need. Believing our own special invisible presence is the *only* guide, and that we must convert others to it, sometimes as forcibly as through murder, defies any guidance or good that this concept could have. And that seems to happen every day in this world. Even Buddhism, which has a strong baseline of committing no harm to others in its teachings, has been co-opted in such places as Myanmar by totalitarian governments to oppress Muslim minorities.

I'm not an expert on religion or a scientist. I am, however, someone who has been deeply harmed by religion and who has had to reconcile the beliefs I grew up around with the harm they caused in my life. Spirituality is an important part of human life, and to cut ourselves off completely from it due to the harm caused by religion is to cut ourselves off from a large part of human experience. Many people claim that transgender people are beyond the bounds of religion, against it. They say it is something we cannot have. I disagree.

My own path to reconciliation on this has been to synthesize some of the beliefs I was taught as a child with a kind of paganism rooted in cultural beliefs of my ancestors and the places they are from. Italian witchcraft has provided me with a framework for taking and leaving what I choose of a tradition that caused me so much harm it nearly killed me and cut me off from spirituality for decades of my life.

Syncretism, to me, is how people oppressed by Christianity make the best of what they're given without giving up their actual tradition. Though many see it as an erasure, I view it as an act of resistance. It's true that since I began studying Italian folk traditions, there has been a measure of peace in my life, a feeling of order and right in the universe. Maybe this sense that there is something bigger than us that keeps our lives from wheeling completely off track is what people of all religions find peace and joy in. This is something that, at least a little, makes sense to me: the notion that we are *not* in control of the big picture (which we can't even see), but someone or something benevolent is. There is a level of submission here that I believe all religions address, to give up one's fallible human design and put one's faith in the idea that there is a much greater one. Even me, with my little kitchen altars and my ancestor altar: I believe in something that is beyond just me through them.

◼

I have always thought a lot about a meditation that Buddhist monk Thich Nhat Hanh describes in his book *Being Peace*. He talks about using washing dishes as a meditation. He describes how the *thought* of washing dishes often gives him pause, but the *act* of washing dishes is always pleasurable: the hot, soapy water, the cleansing. Later, in another article, Hanh described washing dishes at the first monastery he lived at, how the water had to be boiled, how the industrial-sized pots had to be scrubbed. Buddhism promises release from earthly things, but Hanh seems to often use the difficult side of his experiences to create joy when those experiences are less difficult. In fact, in his book *Being Peace*, he likens washing each dish to washing a newborn baby Buddha. I think about this a lot as I wash dishes, hoping to give the care and attention to each that I would such a blessed corporeal form. Often, I fail in this, rush through. But sometimes I do pause and enjoy the warmth of the water, the streak of cleanliness the soapy scrubbing pad provides across each dish.

I have also begun to hand grind my own coffee every morning for my French press. The grinder operates by cranking a handle in a circle and takes probably about five to ten minutes of grinding to get enough for a cup or two of coffee from the French press. This has a really lovely effect on coffee drinking in my life. When I drink my cup in the morning, I usually drink one sole cup, and enjoy it from start to finish. I don't want to repeat the grinding after it is finished, so my purpose in that one cup is to enjoy it as much as possible. When I buy a cup of coffee at a coffee shop, I sip the warm liquid with a gratitude I never had before I hand ground my own coffee beans in the morning. By doing something in a difficult way, we can rejoice in the time when it is either done for us or done in an easier way. The chaotic nature of my life prior to finding a way to joy that works for me is yet another example of this.

.

As a child, I prayed every night, I went to classes in my church's basement, I went to confession and did my penance every week. Despite all these things, through the messages I received both from community and church leaders, I got the "knowledge" that who I was as a queer and trans person was somehow worse than the Christian concept of original sin, something we are all born with, which can be wiped away by baptism and belief in God. Only a few years ago, the Pope described transgender people as "nuclear weapons." Much of the Catholic Church believes transgender people are trying to "undo" God's will by altering our bodies and presentations. "God doesn't make mistakes," is a common rebuke of the idea of transness within the Christian denomination.

Italian folk tradition not only provided me with a way of reclaiming that which I had been taught, but also gives a sly wink at tradition: what the Pope doesn't know won't hurt him, much like when we bless our fortune telling cards under the new moon, so the Madonna doesn't see our blasphemy.

I can't provide a path for others to follow towards this same reconciliation. My own spiritual path, however, does provide me with a sense of order, both in my day-to-day life, and the greater universe. To look to the elements of the earth around me, to look to tradition and belief as it existed for ancestors who came before me—those are things that help me make sense of the world in a way that I assume many people find in organized religions.

I can't give you a path for how I did this all. It's worth saying that again. But that was never what I intended to do here. I can tell you what I've done, I can tell you the things I tried first that failed. I can tell you how I, as an individual, picked up the shipwreck of my life, which I have done before, but never quite in the way I have this time. I no longer lose myself into states I can't control. I no longer wake up every day wishing I hadn't. The nightmares have stopped. I still can't control the leaves on the trees, I still can't make the rain stop falling. It's not that sort of magic—if that sort of magic exists at all. It's a quieter kind, a kind whose only real evidence is a life that finally feels worth living.

ACKNOWLEDGMENTS

Thanks first and foremost to my incredible agent, Nat Kimber, who not only supported the writing and sale of this book but supported me as a friend through the experiences written about in this book. Nat is the rarest and best kind of agent—one who is savvy and smart about the business, kind and caring to the humans on all sides of it, and a true believer in art and its magic. To many, many more years of making magic in the world around us, Nat.

Thanks to my editor and publisher, Dan Simon. The day I sold *All City* to Seven Stories Press, Dan called me to tell me that SSP would like to be my ongoing publisher, that everyone there believed in and supported me and my writing. I can be cynical about the book world, but Dan has proven over and over through the years that he really meant it, and for that rare belief in an industry so often looking for a big splash bestseller right away, I am so very grateful. This thanks extends to everyone at Seven Stories, past and present—Allison, Silvia, Lauren, Ruth, James, Stewart, Tal, Sanina, and all the other people who work tirelessly to bring excellent, progressive work into the world. Thank you to Hannah Mannochio for the book's cover art.

Thanks to Vivien J. Ryder for being consistently there for me in so many ways: as a friend, as someone who gives me advice, as someone who often sees my life more clearly than I can myself. Long live St. Vivien!

Thanks to Sarah, Rob, Bella, and Wyatt Baker. Sarah, I promise that for maybe the first time in my life, the enormous love you give is something I can appreciate as well as it should be appreciated.

Thanks to Sandra Lambert, Christian Morales, and Jason Harris, who read early versions of this essay collection and provided valuable feedback.

Enormous thanks to Ron Kuby, who, despite the fact that I've only ever been able to pay him in whiskey and paperbacks, has appointed himself counsel for my many, many questionable decisions and legal troubles. Ron has become like family over the years, and it's always great to have someone in your corner who knows that you won't listen to a cliché (*pick your battles*), but you will listen to one tailored to you (*every Nazi deserves a punch, but not every Nazi is worth the real cost of that punch*).

All the thanks to every person who donated to the GoFundMe I set up for my legal defense when my rapist sued me. I thought long and hard about the reality of taking $10K from the community around me to fight this battle, but in the end, the decision was made for me by everyone's kindness and generosity. The fact that so many people supported me and my efforts to fight back meant the world to me, and it still does.

Thanks to actor, acting coach, and friend Ken Schatz, who, through letting me sit in on one of his method acting classes and perform Martha from *Who's Afraid of Virginia Woolf?*, taught me that feelings aren't going to kill me—a lesson that's served me well as a writer, an artist, and a human.

The arts organizations of the state of Ohio were extremely generous to me when I was living there. To that end, I thank the Ohioana Book Awards for shortlisting *All City* for their 2020 fiction category, and The Ohio Arts Council, for granting me a 2022 Individual Excellence Award. Some of this book was written in the time that award bought me from daily labor. Unfortunately, the current atmosphere of the state of Ohio—including the lack of anti-SLAPP laws that allowed my rapist to harass me for a year with a frivolous and retaliatory court case for writing about my experience as a survivor, the laws that criminalize abortion, the lack of punishment for police officers who murder innocent Black children, and the laws designed to bar trans people from public life—means that no matter how hard Ohio arts organizations try, they will be less likely to retain queer and trans artists, women artists, BIPOC artists, or artists who are survivors of sexual violence. No arts organization, grant, or award can make Ohio a safe place for minority artists to live and thrive.

This book is in conversation with many other excellent books that I would be remiss to not mention here. Please, if you enjoyed *Breaking the Curse*, read Elissa Washuta's *White Magic*, Hillary Leftwich's *Aura*, Mary-Grace Fahrun's *Italian Folk Magic*, Mallorie Vaudoise's *Honoring Your Ancestors*, Dee Norman's *Burn a Black Candle*, and the works of St. Hildegard of Bingen. (Additional thanks to Elissa for responding so kindly to my fan mail, and Hillary for your unbelievable kindness and support, and for your guidance.) My wish for everyone reading is to find their own magic true to who they are and who their ancestors have been. The amazing tapestry that you are of those who have come before you deserves to be honored, and these books and books like them may help you find your way to that.

Thanks to Sawyer Lovett, who, without a second thought on the matter, put me and Roxy up for a month when I got to Philly. I'm sure I was a pain in the ass to live with, but you handled it admirably. Thanks for the proof that some dudes are, in fact, awesome.

Shout-out to the amazing women in my life, specifically Michelle Brotman, Sabrina Ramouk, Mia Mikowicz, Tara Zavada, Larisse Mondok, Marzi Margo, and Xan Schwartz, for being the support I always need. I hope I give you back even half of what you give me, which is so much more than I'd ever dream of asking for. Your years of consistent support mean the world to me.

Finally, to those struggling with suicidal ideation—I never thought life would get better in the twenty years I struggled with this curse. Life was unbearably gray for so long, and I never thought the clouds would lift. All joy came with heartbreak, and all happiness and success felt empty. But I promise you that you possess the ability to heal, and I am praying to all my deities and ancestors that you find it in yourself. All of you, no matter who you are. You deserve to find your way to the light.